From
Dad & Mom
1976

the
motorcycle
world

THE MOTORCYCLE WORLD
by Phil Schilling

Douglas Wharton Mellor

A Ridge Press Book

Random House

Editor-in-Chief: Jerry Mason
Editor: Adolph Suehsdorf
Art Director: Albert Squillace
Managing Editor: Moira Duggan
Associate Editor: Mimi Gold
Associate Editor: Barbara Hoffbeck
Art Associate: Nancy Louie
Art Associate: David Namias
Art Production: Doris Mullane

Library of Congress Cataloging in Publication Data

Schilling, Phil.
    The motorcycle world.
    "A Ridge Press Book."
    1. Motorcycles. 2. Motorcycling. I. Title
TL440.S32   629.22'75   74-4322
ISBN 0-394-49381-8
Printed and bound in Italy by Mondadori Editore, Verona.

contents

INTRODUCTION

This book touches seventy years of motorcycling. It is neither a history of the sport nor an encyclopedia of models. Even armies of historians can only re-create bits of the past, and not every motorcycle built is worth remembering. Besides, writers who talk a language of bore-and-stroke dimensions don't necessarily convey the real excitement.

This book is an interpretation of past and present. It is an attempt to make sense of the past, to understand why the machinery and the sport grew in certain patterns, and to examine the results of that development. Truly great machines and memorable events lie inside these pages.

Almost all books are based, in part at least, on intellectual larceny and cross-infusion. Scores of enthusiasts provided resources for both text and photographic materials. In England Jim Greening, Jeff Clew, and Robert F. Currie aided in the preparation of the text and the search for photographs, and The National Motor Museum at Beaulieu came to the aid of yet another motorsports book.

Here in the United States, Emmett Moore and Brownie Betar were links to the early days of motorcycling and the adventures of the Indian company. Duane Unkefer and T. C. Bolfert at the Harley-Davidson Motor Company in Milwaukee opened the doors to the factory library and basement; Dick O'Brien shared his recollections and firsthand experience. Dick Klamfoth brought American racing in the 1950's and 1960's into focus, while Kel Carruthers recounted road racing on three continents. Kevin Cameron detailed his paddock life, lived between lunchbag and toolbox. Roger Hull at *Road Rider* Magazine rediscovered the Roy Kerle manuscript and made it available with photographs. Dennis Caprio organized and researched with Kel Carruthers. Richard Renstrom, who sent photos from his personal files, combed factual miscues out of the galley proofs.

Without *Cycle* Magazine, this book would have had some other author. Tom Sargent, *Cycle*'s Publisher, and Cook Neilson, the Editor, engineered the necessary leave-of-absence. They will recognize herein many issues and topics discussed at length. Gordon Jennings unfailingly supplied anecdotes and advice. Jess Thomas, Dale Boller, and Dave Holeman likewise gave their thoughtful counsel.

Doug Mellor literally rearranged his life for three months in order to photograph motorcycles for this volume. He needed the savvy of a detective and the persistence of a bill collector in order to locate some machines. His special photography is a lasting tribute to his industry and impressive talent. Vince Lisanti, Bill Delaney, David Gooley, and Jaydie Putterman all added their first-rate camera craft.

In the end, this book rests on seventy years of motorcycling—lived by many, remembered by others, and researched by a few. That long drama reaches you, the reader, through one mind and one set of words. The past, of course, is only conscious by grace of the writer. So if heresies there be here, I cheerfully accept them as my own.   —P.A.S.

New York City

1.

THE MAGIC MACHINES

Motorcycling teetered at the brink but never toppled. In the beginning, motorcycles scrapped with automobiles in the transportation business, and the automobiles shoveled out grave sites for the bikes. The model T Ford officiated in the United States after World War I; in Europe minicars torpedoed motorcycles in the decade following World War II. Matched against an automobile, the solo motorcycle lacked at least three important features: two wheels and an all-weather roof. A motorcycle outfitted with a sidecar provided a third wheel, and in some cases a top. Nevertheless, in the transport trade drivers and passengers demanded their comfort. When it was raining, they wished to be dry; when cold, warm; when hot, cool; when dusty, clean. Early mechanical contraptions, with two wheels or four, allowed the elements to brutalize occupants. Automobiles moved swiftly to enclosed bodies. The sealed coachwork well served an age which believed that sanitation and civilization formed an inseparable union.

Had it not been for motorcycle enthusiasts, the machines would have vanished. Museums might have collected them as curios of an early mechanical age, and sandwiched two-wheelers between crystal radio sets and straight-edge razors. That didn't happen. Enthusiasts ignored the weather and learned to ignore all those dreary, limp jokes. Enthusiasts knew why motorcycling wouldn't disappear. And the wind-in-the-hair, bugs-in-the-teeth rubbish had little to do with it.

Motorcycling generates a sense of mastery in the rider. In a way motorcycles are incompetent: They can't stand up by themselves. The very act of balancing and guiding such a vehicle creates a union. Out of this unconscious telegraphy between bike and rider a sense of mastery begins to grow. Beyond the simple union of balance, the motorcycle telegraphs the rider in never-ending streams. The impulses flow back through handlebars, footpegs, and saddle. When braking, the rider's body inches forward in the saddle; loads feed into his arms and wrists; he feels weight in his shoulders. If he squeezes the front-brake lever a bit harder, the loads through his arms instantly build. Banking into a corner, the bars, pegs, and saddle can light up with messages: A peg skims the tarmac, a tiny wag momentarily flutters the bars, and saddle-jerks record rear-tire slip. Surrounded by rushing wind and the engine's mechanical thrashing, the rider speaks a body language with his machine and the road below. Nothing need be lost or filtered out. This body-talk, a kind of nonverbal language which man and machine carry on, proceeds directly.

All motorcycles are not created equal. Some machines correspond with riders in slurs, while others send loud, precise messages. And not every rider listens equally well through the seat of his pants. Indeed, most motorcyclists never reach a full measure of correspondence with their machine. Telegraphic chatter at the outer edge of adhesion doesn't draw the everyday enthusiast. He can be satisfied with something less, because on any motorcycle at almost any speed the messages remain audible. The motorcycle responds and reports, again and again. That's half the magic.

Motorcyclists have a ritual of washing and tinkering. This activity holds a clue to another kind of magic about motorcycles. Observe the Saturday-morning ceremony. The motorcyclist polishes, then repolishes, the gas cap. He discovers a loose nut, and retightens it, with a faint trace of satisfaction. The motorcyclist walks around his bike, pushing and pulling on levers and pedals, watching the mechanisms operate. He is a switch-clicker, snapping the headlight-beam switch from high to low, listening to the snick and feeling the spring-loaded lever roll over center. At times the motorcyclist just looks at his bike, not an idle, out-of-focus view, but a studied gaze which moves from one piece of its hardware to the next.

Opening pages: The 1916 Indian
Powerplus with optional sidecar
was elegant transportation.
On nippy days the chair sheltered
the passenger; the rider at
least had mitts. Below: In 1914
the soloist's Harley-Davidson shows
the last vestiges of
bicycling: foot pedals and crank.

*Below: Motorcycles, no matter how
modern, always appear as
assemblages of separate parts. That
happy honesty resides behind
the nose of a 1973 Kawasaki roadracer
as well as in the handshift lever
of a 1930 Harley-Davidson or in the
lever gates for clutch
and gearbox on a 1928 Henderson.*

Below: Motorcycle components have a timeless classic quality, despite well-advertised yearly advances. The front brake belongs to a 1961 Ducati F3, the direct kick-starter system and speedometer are pieces to a 1916 Powerplus Indian. Early machines wore their engineering solutions outside, in full view.

Motorcyclists are lovers of nuts and bolts. They have a passion for things mechanical. Motorcycles can seduce hardware lovers because they radiate a machine-quality. Machine, motorcycle—the words interchange freely. That kind of word-swapping works with classic devices such as Bugattis; there nothing hides behind slick, gratuitous covers. The machine label, however, won't stick to Chevrolet Biscaynes.

Motorcycles are classic mechanical things. If not constant, the motorcycle form has remained recognizable. The locations of the main pieces have shifted little since 1915. Although space limitations prevent much gross experimentation, the traditional form can't stand much tampering anyway, perhaps in part for nonengineering reasons. Motor scooters may be the most rationalized and streamlined kind of two-wheeled vehicles, yet motorcyclists scorn the scooter's mechanical credentials and ridicule its smooth exterior. There have been attempts to

streamline and style motorcycles, but such packaging has always courted disaster with enthusiasts. A motorcycle can't be cowled in sheetmetal. The engine must look like an engine; a good portion of the tube framing must be visible; the wheels should be open. All components must be in their proper place. Adherence to form is required.

As the twentieth century turns into its final quarter, lovers of nuts and bolts feel cheated. Accelerating technology piles mystery upon mystery inside contrivances which surround, serve, and victimize us. This invisible technology first perplexes, later overwhelms us. Consider the transistor: It neither moves nor glows nor hums. It is just there, working with faceless anonymity and cold efficiency.

In the case of classic machines, you can tell how something works. You watch it, catch it in the act. Movement, especially traceable movement, makes a process self-explanatory and comprehensible: Lever A pivots on ful-

Motorcycle enthusiasts in two time frames. Left: At a rally and gypsy tour held in Atlanta, Georgia, in 1950. Below: More than twenty years later, the cloth-cap decorations had given away to jacket-patch jungles. And motocross, unknown in American motorcycling of 1950, was the rage of the early 1970's.

Telegraphic communication between rider and machine increases at the edge. Roadracing, motocross, fast street riding, international trials, or dirt-track racing—all challenge the rider's skill at body-talking with a piece of hardware at human and mechanical limits.

crum B and pulls rod C. These visible relationships touch our understanding. One can grasp an idea in its elemental state and can see the solution as the designer originally saw it—before the idea was later sent to committee, refined, developed, electrified, hydraulicized, transistorized, and sanitized. Motorcycles, even modern ones, remain simple machines. They still make sense on the lever A/rod C level: Watch it move, see it work—simple, direct, satisfying. And that's why motorcycle enthusiasts celebrate Saturday mornings with hose and hand tools.

Contemporary motorcyclists descend from tinkers. Very early riders had few choices. They either dealt with problems or walked away from them. If the first-generation motorcyclist elected to fumble toward a solution, he might have taken his counsel from a general manual, such as H. Corbishley's *Motor cycles and Sidecars*, tucked away in a toolbox or stuffed in the sidecar until summoned forth by strange occurrences.

"**Engine Noise**—Immediate attention should be paid to any unusual noises, whether they appear to come from the engine or some other part of the machine. Frequently their cause can be determined by their period, that is the number of times the noise is heard relative to the movements of certain parts of the engine or machine; thus in the case of a noise that occurs with each revolution of the road wheels, attention should be directed to the possibility of something fouling these. Lack of oil may cause a harsh rumbling noise in the engine."

An observant ear and the manual might spare an engine and its owner some catastrophe. But it took a discerning ear, tuned for diagnosis:

"Worn main bearings will cause a sort of hollow rumbling, probably accentuated at high speeds. Loose big ends give rise to a sort of thud, usually more or less constant, but if the thud develops into a rattle at increased speeds the bearing should be seen to at once. Wear on the gudgeon pin is evidenced by sharp metallic taps, sounding something like an overheated engine; but the noise does not cease when the spark is retarded. . . . Piston slap or rattle is, as the term implies, due to a piston being a too easy fit in the cylinder. It may best be described as a clattering sort of noise. On a worn engine it may be that several of these noises are combined."

When bright sunny days grew sullen with rainclouds, and firm dry roads dissolved into mud, the pioneering motorcyclist might consult the manual, hoping to correct a suddenly rough-running engine. The manual wasn't always the best reading for a steady downpour.

"The problem of perfect carburetion is a very complex one and as yet unsolved, for it is dependent on so many factors. The chief difficulty which presents itself is the constantly varying speed of the engine and the load. A certain mixture of petrol vapour and air is only suitable for an engine running at a certain speed and with a certain load, and should the load vary, the mixture should also be altered to suit the new conditions. Up to the present it has not been found possible to make an instrument which would produce the necessary alteration exactly, and the best carburetting system is, therefore, merely a compromise. Other complications introduced are the temperatures of the air and of the engine, density of the atmosphere, and quality of fuel."

Given such troubles, the enthusiast and his machine formed a union of misery. His willingness to endure a sometimes truculent contraption testified to the motorcycle's power of attraction. Training in adversity has always served the certified enthusiast well. Often he's had a lot to explain. For example: why water, running down one's back and draining off into the bottom of one's boots, isn't all that bothersome; why carnival riders, buzzing around inside wooden dromes or steel cages, belong to freak shows and not motorcycling; why motorcycles really aren't that dangerous; why motorcycling isn't a little suspect or even subversive.

Explanations have been more easily understood in England and Western Europe than in America. Most riders—as opposed to enthusiasts—had come off pedal bikes and were working their way toward automobiles. Any keenness for motorcycles related more to a weariness from pedaling than the excitement of motorcycling. Two-wheelers (and three-) may have left the nonsporting rider cold, wet, and drafty enough so that he might question what real merit motorcycles held. Yet at minimum, the garden-variety cyclist in England and Europe had his own experience which hinted at motorcycling's excitement. In America the motoring public skipped two-wheelers during the interwar period and planted itself inside Detroit creations. The four-wheeled citizenry had more accusations than questions for motorcyclists. Such a mood fit nineteen-twenties America, which mass-produced readymade heroes and villains. A country that fretted through the Red Scare and lionized Charles Lindbergh loved winners and majorities, distrusted losers and minorities. Motorcycles floated outside the mainstream. That fact kept motorcycle men on the defensive.

Where motorcycle enthusiasts congregated, disputes eventually ensued. So it has been from the start. Hot words crackle between warm friends over bikes. An enthusiast, loyal to a brand, exposes himself to roasting criticism from his motorcycling pals. He shields himself from this heat by knowing as much as possible about his machine, its vices and virtues. Critics force a loyalist to defend his choice as an intelligent pick. The boundaries of dispute stretch and widen: singles, twins, or multis; types of suspension components; speeds; acceleration figures; weights—and on into the night. Arguments get spun around, and discussions enter yet another field. This on-going dialogue continues, day after day, week after week, so perhaps

there's a deeper reason for all this bike-talk. Motorcycle enthusiasts not only resell themselves on their choices, but also reaffirm their interest in the sport.

Lively discussions over motorcycles sometimes end on a race course. Motorcycles have always been performance machines, and racing is a natural, logical arm of a sport which trades on rapid point-to-point performance. Motorcyclists have discovered or invented all kinds of contests, ranging from motordrome riding to transcontinental dashes to motocross racing. Factories have supported racing from the outset, but manufacturers have gone in and out of racing like transients through revolving doors. Some makers have stayed close to the spinning axis and hung on, while others have quickly come full circle and jettisoned.

That hoary proposition, "racing improves the breed," has its partisans in motorcycling, though truth would better be served by observing that racing promotes the brand. For manufacturers, racing can be a gigantic bill-board operation, carried out with professional riders and advertising space. The backbone of racing, however, doesn't connect through the hired guns of manufacturers. Rather, weekend amateurs—competing almost in sandlot fashion—build the vital spine. Even pros started unpaid.

Fun is the code word for weekend racers. Whatever the form, racing possesses the magic of motorcycling, but in a hypersensitive, hyperactive state. Competition motorcycles not only communicate more keenly with the rider, the machinery contains more engineering tricks. Fun for the weekend racer lives at the edge, which divides the last reliable horsepower from the next crippled one, which runs between the correct tire and the best one for a changing dirt-track groove, which separates the last bit of traction from a breakaway slide; which cuts between all the good choices and the few brilliant ones. Fun is honing a sharp edge on the hardware, and then at speed—wired into the machine's telegraphy—body-talking toward the limit.

2.

Cannonball Baker was a cloud of dust rolling east across California. It was May, 1914, three months before Europe slid into the Great War. With the Pacific Ocean at his back, Baker—christened Erwin G. but nicknamed Cannonball—gunned his two-speed twin-cylinder Indian toward New York City and the Atlantic. Cannonball: The name captured the man. He was on his way to a transcontinental record. Baker had been born with a gift for endurance and grew up with a taste for adventure. A big, lean, lanky fellow, Baker made an amazing discovery after he bought his first motorcycle. He had endurance and stamina that left his motorcycling pals wilted and exhausted behind him. "I found it an easy matter to ride a great deal further and faster in a day without fatigue than the ordinary rider."

Not a man to rush into a transcontinental crossing unprepared, Baker had trained. For starters, beginning in 1912, he rode straight through from Indianapolis to Miami Beach, Florida. Then he grabbed a steamer to Havana, chugged all over Cuba, then Jamaica, took a ship to the Isthmus of Panama, crossed it on his motorcycle and sailed to California. By the time he reached San Diego, he had ridden some 14,000 miles. In California and Arizona more miles rolled under his wheels as he competed in endurance runs and road races.

Conditioning wasn't enough. Given the tracks that passed for roads in 1914, a trans-American dash could easily be rained out. After months of study, Baker and a government weather clerk formulated a plan which would place Cannonball between bad-weather fronts moving east. Baker considered two routes, and picked the shorter, tougher one. Two months of hard detail work began: ". . . we started in to write letters to people along this route, inquiring about roads and bridges and where gasoline could be located. We found that from Rice to Fort Apache [Arizona] it was impossible to get gasoline. The places were located from 40 to 120 miles from railroad stations,

so we arranged to have gasoline packed in on burros from the railroad station to the various points on the desert and mountain trails, which cost me seventy cents a gallon."

At last all the pieces fell together. "The morning of May 3 found me dressed in leather riding trousers, short raincoat and khaki shirt, while I had had a special canteen made to hold a gallon of water to help me cross the desert." At 9 A.M. Baker left.

As he highballed his V-twin eastward, Baker's experiences traced out an America which had just pushed itself out of the nineteenth century. The United States had almost become embroiled in a second Mexican-American war by occupying Vera Cruz in April, 1914, so the southern border was tense in May. Outside San Diego, Cannonball met a regiment of U.S. infantry marching along the Mexican border. "This road where I met them was in a mountain pass and they formed in line and gave me just enough room to pass through them on the mountain trail, all cheering and waving their hands. About five miles further on I came on to another body of soldiers, who were at rest. It certainly did seem as if war had begun with the Mexicans, for it looked as if the boys had enough cannon and ammunition to blow up the whole of Mexico."

Baker had his own concerns. Thirst was one. Frequent stops to drink would delay him, so he resorted to an old Indian trick. He placed a dime-sized pebble under his tongue and held it there, mile after mile. At the end of his first day, a sandstorm chased him all the way to the Santa Fe railroad tracks. From there it was easy; he rode the tracks sixty-four miles into Yuma.

On his second day out, Baker was hurrying along in Arizona, a state which had been in the Union only two years. He crossed the Castle Dome Mountains, and then dropped into a bad stretch of desert "made up of rocky gulches, deep washes, and quantities of sand, all the while through intense heat. Four miles before reaching the

OMING!"

Opening pages: The 1907 Merkel
Light was a half-step away
from bicycling; it had
a crank-and-chain for starting and
assisting the single-cylinder
engine up grades.
Below: Cannonball Baker poses with
a 7-hp Indian V-twin without
the Spring-Cradle Frame.

town of Agua Caliente (called Water Springs by the natives), I ran out of gasoline while in deep sand, and from there I had to push my machine along until I reached the Springs, with the thermometer standing at 119 degrees in the shade."

Civilization had not tranquilized the Wild West completely by 1914. On the third day, Baker's friends in Phoenix laughed at his "pop-gun" sidearm. ". . . Doc Bordeau stepped up to me and took the toy away and snapped a real 'cannon' on my handlebars—a Smith & Wesson .38 cal. long, for which I was mighty glad afterward. The gun looked all right to me because it had three notches on the butt of it. It proved afterward that I sure did have use for this gun, for while coming through the Indian reservation at Fort Apache I was given a big welcome by more dogs than Indians, and I had to put this gun to use. These dogs are worse than wolves, and I had to drop two of them in their tracks in order to get by."

Baker rolled on. Between Phoenix and Springerville, Arizona, he churned forward in hot desert sands 250 feet below sea level, wound his way up narrow, dangerous cliff roads, and tracked through mountain snow at 9,650 feet above sea level. By the time he reached Albuquerque, Baker thought the toughest part of the trip, his Great Desert crossing, was behind him. But later, outside Santa Fe, after eighty-six miles of mountain climbing, a swollen mountain stream barred the road and nearly scratched his record attempt. Baker spent all day locating a place to ford—without totally immersing the motorcycle. He finally pushed the bike through the water and resumed the journey.

Outside Dodge City, Kansas, though on "good roads," he fixed one flat tire after another: six nails in twenty miles. Near Ellsworth, Kansas, a big shepherd dog tackled his machine. "This dog seemed to have a great desire for the Goodyear tire on my front wheel, but my desire was still greater. The dog took a fall out of me which

put me in bad shape, as I slid along the road on my elbows and knees. I kept the tire and the dog lost his life. At Ellsworth I had a good meal, then sent for a doctor to get bandaged up, and went to bed."

Near Casey, Illinois, Baker blasted along, trying to avoid a terrific thunderstorm. "I knew I never would get through even with a team of horses over the mudholes if I was caught in heavy rain." Baker got wet, but he escaped the worst of the downpour.

Indiana: "Being a native of Indiana, everyone was out to welcome me, and the message was sent along the way: 'Clear the road, I am a-coming.' "

Ohio: "The boys in Columbus . . . finally led me to the end of the beautiful pavements . . . and, as if chopped off by a knife, came the end of that good road. Before me lay roads that looked like newly plowed fields, and I found on getting into them that it was mud almost knee-deep."

Pennsylvania: "I . . . covered a distance of 232.8 miles through rain and mud. . . ."

New Jersey: ". . . we started for New York, and it being a very dark night, we were lost two or three times even with the [guide] rider who knew the roads. He showed me the way to Weehawken, N.J., where I took the ferry to New York City."

New York: "My race with time was then ended . . . my trip had taken only 11 days, 12 hours and 10 minutes. . . . Then after talking with reporters until 2 o'clock in the morning, I turned in."

The machine which carried Cannonball Baker 3,379 miles across the continent represented the progressive wing of motorcycle orthodoxy as practiced in America. His mount, a stock and standard Indian machine, wasn't a lashed-up, beefed-up pedal-bicycle tailored to hold an engine. The machine was a motorcycle, with the engine and frame designed as complementary pieces, a real gearbox located behind the engine, a full suspension system, and electric lights. The engine was a narrow-angle V-twin, displacing 61 cubic inches or 1,000 cubic centimeters. The valves were located in a side pocket of the combustion chamber—the inlet valve overhead, the exhaust below, and the sparkplug between. Such valve configuration was quite common; detachable heads weren't.

Indian did not cast the cylinder head integral with the cylinder itself. Removable heads made it convenient to decarbonize piston tops and combustion chambers, and separate heads made grinding valves less of a chore. Decarbonizing and valve work received a good deal of attention in the early days of motorcycling; that had much to do with the quality of oil, engine materials, carburetion accuracy, and lubrication systems.

On Indian's big V-twin, the engine's lubrication was a divided task: A hand-operated plunger-pump supplemented the mechanical oil pump. Thus, when the engine was operating under severe load, crawling uphill, or cracking along near full throttle, the rider gave the engine an extra shot of oil with the hand pump. If the rider were derelict in his oiling duties, the engine could overheat, seize, damage valves, and destroy bearings. An overly eager pump hand, however, would have the engine blowing out a blue haze of oil smoke, a sure sign that the rider was headed for a premature task of decarbonizing. Most early engines had total-loss oiling; the excess oil either went out the exhaust pipe or settled in the bottom of the crankcase, or both. The rider drained out the crankcase oil puddle at suitable intervals. Then he scraped out the carbon deposits which had formed on the pistons and in the heads. Even though one might be blessed with an unfailingly accurate pump hand, other problems could force a look inside the engine under the heads; for example, the uncertainties of carburetion might produce very well-done and leaky valves. Detachable heads were good things.

Baker's record-setter had no bicycle pedals. In the very beginning, bicycle cranks were essential since many motorcycles had only one gear and no clutch. A dual-drive system prevailed. The rider could turn the rear wheel by pedaling bicycle-style, and the rear wheel would crank the engine over for starting. Once under way the rider could rest. Until he stopped. Stopping the machine required squelching the engine; to resume, the engine had to be pedaled back to life. Pedals and hill climbing went together naturally, because early motorcycles with small engines demanded uphill assistance. As engines became more powerful and clutch-and-gearbox systems proliferated, manufacturers fitted kickstarters in place of pedals. Baker's Indian had footboards and a kickstarter.

The addition of two-speed gearboxes was a more dramatic advance than the subtraction of bicycle pedals. Since American motorcycles had to cope with vast differences in terrain, a huge engine was the most straightforward way to create a single-gear machine with a broad speed range. Giant 61-inch chuffers could plow through the rough stuff, and then steam along well-surfaced roads. No matter how large and torquey the engine, single-gear motorcycles were limited. Two-speed gearboxes extended the performance range of monster engines, allowing easier departures from rest, greater climbing capabilities, more flexibility in traffic, plus smoother and faster running.

When makers learned to balance crankshafts more precisely, which helped to damp jerky power pulses, and when they devised better driveline cushioning to buffer out shocks, another hallmark of early motorcycling—belt drives—faded away. Belts were known for their silence and cleanliness; chains meant noise, slinging oil, and the jerks. The main attraction of belts was a kind of elastic characteristic that eased the lurching of early motorcycles. Considering the running roughness, a little belt-slip wasn't a bad thing. But stronger, more even-running engines almost required chain drive, and usually they got it. Only

Cannonball Baker on the Mexican-American border with an Indian Powerplus V-twin in the Spring-Cradle Frame. Baker held a sidecar record for the Three-Flag Run (Canada to Mexico) in the nineteen-teens. His total elapsed time for 1,716 miles stood at 2 days, 17 hours, and 53 minutes.

The 1916 Indian Powerplus had
open cog wheels for the speedometer.
The rear lantern fastened to the vertical
arm, which ran up to the leaf springs.
Below: Headlamps were optional;
the 1918 Powerplus solo
avoided dark nights.
The old V-twin engines took air straight,
without any filtering elements.

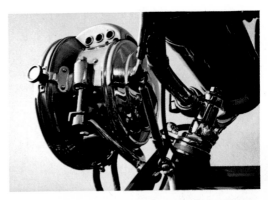

briefly did the makers of Indian motorcycles flirt with belts. Chained power was an Indian trademark.

In New York, Baker testified to his machine's frame. "In my estimation it was the cradle spring frame above all else that contributed to my success. It absorbed all road shocks and vibrations, and this, of course, saved my strength and, besides, enabled me to make speed over the roughest roads." The Hoosier ad man wasn't spinning a web from thin air. The "Cradle-Spring Frame" probably was smoother-riding than its contemporary hard-tailed rigid-framed competitors. With rigid-framed motorcycles, if the seat springs did not sufficiently ease the pounding which abused the rider's body, he stood up on the pegs or floorboards and used his legs as shock absorbers. Motorcycle riders did a lot of standing.

Indian's Cradle-Spring Frame reduced the suffering but didn't eliminate the standing. The frame had swinging-arm rear suspension, though it differed from modern practice. The swinging-arm hinged to the central frame on one end and held the rear wheel at the other. Instead of coil springs and dampers rising vertically from the bosses on the swinging arm, a vertical rear fork looped up and connected to two leaf springs which were disposed horizontally and joined the central frame under the saddle. Indians had the inside track on fully sprung frames. Most makers remained loyal to rigid frames and saved their creativity for front suspensions. Manufacturers showed a dazzling number of different combinations. Any concoction of springs, links, forks, and stays might show up on the front of a motorcycle. Indian mounted the wheel hub on trailing links. The movement of the links was controlled by a vertical fork which attached above the tire to a leaf spring that sprouted forward right below the juncture of the front fork. Despite all public shouting, those Indian leaf springs—front and back—had harsh action and short travel movement. Edwin Baker took his jolts.

Cannonball Baker wrote a message from the Pacific to the Atlantic. Motorcycles had progressed beyond cantankerous toys. Motorcycles were viable machines.

In a way, Indian demonstrated this proposition narrowly. Baker's dash was a partisan stunt on which the Indian concern happily traded. Distance records were never safe when motorcycle makers wanted advertising copy. For this reason, Baker's mark was later broken and rebroken by a succession of riders on various motorcycles. Racing was another kind of public demonstration, and by 1914 Indian motorcycles had already won the Isle of Man Tourist Trophy race, set speed records in Europe and America, and posted victories on board and dirt tracks.

Competition was heated. Harley-Davidson and Excelsior, for two, guaranteed that. But nothing Indian would ever do in the decade after 1910 would match the purity and scale of one man on one motorcycle racing the clock across a continent.

Jack Prince poured excitement into motorcycling, too, though in an entirely different way. Prince was a New Jersey engineer who had the soul of a promoter. Velodrome bicycle racing pulled large crowds into grandstands in the early twentieth century, but Prince had more spectacular blueprints than push-bike racing. Prince engineered small oval board-track speedways which varied in distance from one-quarter to one-third mile around; the largest "motordrome" stretched out to a half-mile. The turns banked steeply to permit high-speed racing, tilting at forty-five to forty-eight degrees, though some motordrome walls tipped sixty degrees. Builders constructed a timber framework which anchored into concrete bases. The actual surface of the track was formed with two-by-four pine boards laid on edge, or with two-by-twos. According to Prince, the tricky part was blending the banking and straightaways smoothly together. Not unsurprisingly, Prince had his own construction methods, which he

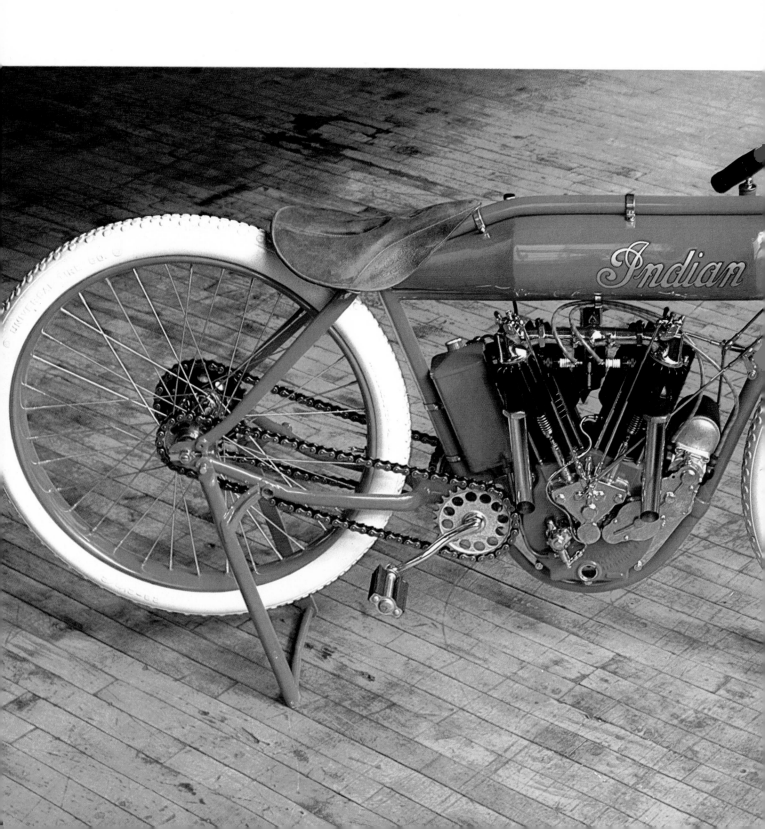

Motordrome racers were spare, hard little machines, barely more than bicycles with enormous 61-cu. in. engines in their holds. Pedal-power starting required right-side chain; the engine drove the rear wheel on the left. A system of rods and cranks controlled the engine from the low handlebars.

claimed eliminated blending irregularities in the surface.

After Prince's first wooden saucer opened in Paterson, New Jersey, in 1908, a spree of motordrome construction followed. Dromes went up in major cities—New York, Philadelphia, Chicago, St. Louis, and Los Angeles, among others. Perhaps it was no accident that these dromes were built in or near amusement parks, since the pocket-sized board tracks sold speed and danger in a compact setting. It was comprehensible racing, and well organized too. Promotors put together the American Motordrome League in which cities fielded home and traveling teams. The teams were professional, and league scores were kept in baseball fashion.

Early motordrome racing seemed safer than racing on small horse tracks which would engulf riders in blinding dust after a few laps. The safety point was debatable because the motordromes had their own peculiar brand of danger. Intense rivalry filled every racing program. There were six or seven events: a couple of heat races, a final event, match races between team captains or the quickest riders, handicap and consolation events. The racing stayed incredibly close, and dead-heat finishes weren't unheard-of occurrences. Since motordrome racing was team racing and handlebar-to-handlebar racing, hooking, elbowing, and bumping made up the finer points of good inside fighting. Officials often winked at those deadly tactics. But the most lethal development in motordrome racing was the most inevitable one: Speeds shot up as the competition stiffened.

Indian and Excelsior waged a battle of racing technology with their 61-cu. in. V-twin engines. The first Indian drome racers had engines which were not substantially different from the unit in Cannonball Baker's record-breaker. The engine, which was dropped into a spindly rigid frame, accounted for most of the bike's 175-pound racing weight. The motorcycle rolled on 28-inch tires

*Motordrome racing was close,
intense, and often bloody. Morty Graves
(left), the Flying Merkel jockey,
battles with Al Ward in a match race at
the old Los Angeles Coliseum
in 1910. The one-third-mile drome was a
Jack Prince project completed
in 1909. That year the lap speeds
approached 90 mph on the board saucer.*

pumped up to 100 pounds per square inch. From its dropped handlebars to its frail tubing, the drome racer looked like a racing bicycle built around an enormous V-twin engine. The earliest twins might have delivered 10 or 12 horsepower at the rear wheel; that was strong enough to produce speeds in excess of 80 mph. As drome racing became more competitive, Indian—the biggest name in the field—dropped development of the old inlet-over-exhaust V-twin and struck out at Excelsior with special eight-valve V-twins which had clutches and two-speed gearboxes. The bikes, with their spaghetti-gauge frame tubes, remained delicate, but they were far more powerful and therefore faster. Laps in the nineties became commonplace.

As speed escalated so did danger. The speeds on the banks subjected the plucky riders and eggshell motorcycles to tremendous down forces which could cause tires to rupture and riders to faint. The surface reserved cruel punishment for riders who fell off. They collected a hideful of splinters. Some racers suited up in heavy silk underwear, thinking that silk would help turn away splinters. Heads were more vulnerable than hides. Racers had nothing to protect them from concussions. The mixed bag of headwear—everything from cloth and leather caps to aviator helmets—might fend off a few pine splinters, but did nothing to reduce serious concussive blows.

The track surface could not be planed and polished like a basketball court because the motorcycles needed a rough surface to get any traction at all out of the hard, narrow tires. The rough boards soaked up oil, and this left the track very dodgey. The oil came out of the motorcycles: Every time a rider hand-pumped, an oil cloud spat out the exhaust stubs and settled on the track. Worse than a slick plank was a broken one. Planks could break, leaving a board cocked up in the face of on-rushing traffic; hitting one head-on could deck a bike instantly.

Although the increasing speeds aggravated all

the characteristic motordrome problems, splinter-bowl fans loved the show. The gruesome accidents were heart-stoppers, and eventually the paying customers started to share in the dying. Curious onlookers, standing at the tops of the dromes with their heads bobbing out on the track, invited decapitation if a machine went out of control and slammed into the upper retaining wall. Or bikes might hurtle off the speedway and pitch into the grandstands at 90 mph. Every weekend, it seemed, brought injury or death. The splinter bowls' bloodiest season came in 1913. Motordromes earned their final epithet: murderdromes.

The carnage was too much. Municipal governments began squeezing the dromes shut. Interest waned when the much safer one-mile and two-mile board speedways reached completion. Whatever else, the motordrome madness imprinted motorcycling with a carnival-freak-show stamp, and endowed two-wheelers with a tradition of daredeviltry and ignorant enthusiasm.

After World War I, Jack Prince was back promoting motordromes again. The second time around he met vitriolic opposition from motorcycle spokesmen. Everyone had had enough the first time through. Motorcycling never needed a daredevil motordrome legacy. Thanks to Jack Prince, it got it anyway.

Motordroming didn't fall in a vacuum. American motorcycling began sagging after 1913, when a nose count yielded some forty-odd manufacturers. Though industry sales tapered down and took marginal companies out, Indian, Harley-Davidson, and Excelsior consolidated their position as the giant names in American motorcycling. The industry leader rolled out a new V-twin engine in 1916.

Indian forsook its old inlet-over-exhaust chugger by introducing a 61-cu. in. sidevalve V-twin which they dubbed the "Powerplus." The engine was, as its name suggested, considerably stronger than the first-generation V-twin. The sidevalve flathead engine anticipated the gen-

eral direction of American design. So did the three-speed gearbox. Those riders who wished to risk the mysteries of electric lighting could have it. No one rated "bulb lighting" a new concept, and not many believed it a perfected system either. Reliability counted. Acetylene gas lamps, if not completely dependable and windproof, at least failed in predictable ways and definite steps. Electric lights were

too sly and quick. They worked fine exactly to the moment when they stranded bike and rider in utter darkness.

Even with electric lighting and the optional Cradle-Spring Frame, motorcyclists wouldn't get soft and flabby, especially when starting a Powerplus Indian on a chilly morning. Success demanded knowledge of the drill. Despite its low compression ratio, one couldn't kick the

Early motorcycling had its dangers and mysteries. Spring-loaded foot clutches earned the epithet "suicide clutches"; they would not tolerate rider error. Carburetors imperfectly mixed air and fuel, and these crude instruments were the objects of endless hours of tinkering, adjusting, and cursing.

engine through without raising the exhaust valves for compression release. Rotating the right-hand grip fully retarded the ignition and opened the valves, all by means of rods, universal joints, and levers. There was nothing so crude as a sheath-and-wire cable.

The next step involved priming. One pulled up the knob handle on the gas cap, which drew gasoline into a syringe-type gun that hid under the cap. After removing cap and gun from the gas tank, the rider opened the priming cocks on each cylinder head, squirted raw gas into the cylinders with the gun, closed the cylinder-head cocks, put the gas cap back on, opened the gasoline taps, held down the springloaded float-button on the carburetor for a count of ten, kicked the engine through a couple of times, switched the ignition on, brought the engine to compression, cracked the compression release, and kicked smartly while closing the release. Done properly, the engine would burble into a V-twin cadence; tried otherwise, it would respond with cold silence, save for an occasional pop.

After warm-up, the rider would—in the event of a lady and a sidecar—assist her into the chair. Sidecars were the dearest option one could buy, and the whipping boy of a genuine soloist. But for those motorcycle men who wanted companionship, sidecars provided the answer. Compared to the bone-shattering bolt-on pillion saddles, a sidecar, floating on springs, was civilization itself.

The clutch was hardly as refined. Riders referred to them as suicide clutches. The left foot pedal had a spring return; should the rider stop with the machine in gear, clutch depressed and engine running, he dared not lose his balance or do anything that would accidentally remove his foot from the depressed clutch lever. Sidecar-equipped machines which were stable at rest weren't so touchy or treacherous on this point as solo mounts. No wonder then that the clutch could be operated on the Powerplus with a positive-position hand lever, as well as the springloaded pedal. It made good insurance for those riders with a nervous left foot. The clutch hand lever proved handy in other cases. Were the rider off the machine and pushing his outfit through deep mud, the hand lever was convenient.

Dropping into first required practiced timing. A too-quick thrust did the gears no good, while a cautious move begat gear-grinding agony.

Once under way the gearbox could be moved into third very quickly—at some speed just over a brisk walking pace. The Powerplus had low-down chuffing power, for it certainly didn't rev madly: 2,500 rpm invited the cast-iron pistons to fracture. But within its limits, the Powerplus could lope all day, 40 to 45 mph, should one find a good, long-lasting road.

The dual braking system on the Indian V-twin probably reflected two facts. First, road surfaces aided stopping by placing a low ceiling on road speeds: mud, for example, has great decelerative value. Second, in 1916 there wasn't all that much to hit anyway. The rider's right foot operated the internal shoes of the rear drum brake, while by drawing the hand lever tight he caused an external collar to bite on the outside of the drum. Esoteric, but not too effective. A front brake was a thing of the future.

The Indian Standard model, a Powerplus engine in the Cradle-Spring Frame, was a luxurious sporting motorcycle. If you didn't like the leaf-spring special, then you could opt for the common rigid-framed model. Indian had both alternatives covered. Whatever the frame choice, the optional sidecar allowed the sport to share the luxury —providing the passenger was both petite and game.

How quickly Cannonball Baker had slashed a path across the continent, or how fast a motordrome pilot clicked off a mile, may have concerned the Indian Standard owner very little. Most riders cared how their motorcycle looked and ran and felt. And on these points the big V-twins satisfied.

41

3.

THE LONG ROLL

Once upon a time advertising copy eschewed slogans and spoke in parables. Read today, those parables—commercial rather than religious at bottom—weave a pattern of an earlier life, its problems and desires. The solutions, or resolutions, channeled down to a single answer. From a distance of a half-century, the little stories seem quaint and homey as they meander leisurely toward a final point. Or perhaps it only seems that way to a television generation nurtured on thirty-second hard-sell commercials. Consider the case of Jones, the farm, and a Harley-Davidson, as described in an advertising brochure issued by the cycle manufacturer in 1920:

"Jones worked on a farm and he was feeling blue. Beads of sweat stood on his forehead as he walked beside the rack pitching hay. His thoughts ran back over the last few days and he felt again the heat and the intense unquenched desire for a swim. A beautiful cool lake lay only two miles away—yet it might have been a million, for not once this year had he had the time or energy to walk over in the evening.

"And Sunday, how he had hung around the house—almost no desire to get out—little interest in anything—just loafing around all day. He had sat watching enviously the couples ride by.

"'Aw! what's the use,' he said, 'the people who have the money get the pleasures. I'm tied down to the farm like a man in jail. No way to get out to where there is life—no break in the bars.

"'But there must be some way for me to get enjoyment. I don't want to leave the farm for the city. There must be a way out of this prison of work without pleasure. If I could only find the way.'

"Then one day someone gave Jones a booklet. He wasn't much interested, but he read it through. It told about young men and their friends, and the pleasures they might enjoy at little expense—cool rides in the moonlight

after a grilling day in the fields. It told of swims at far-off beaches brought close with the Harley-Davidson motorcycle. It told of rides to cities—theaters, concerts, fairs—the whole scale of pleasures, all his—and how, if he'd come in we'd explain how to get them.

"'Just what I want,' thought Jones. He came to us and we told him of the Harley-Davidson motorcycle and side car, and the easy payment plan which would bring them within his reach. We showed him how others with less money than he had were paying as they rode and were saving because they rode Harley-Davidsons.

"We broke the bars to Jones' prison."

The story had a faded charm by 1920. The theme of "economical transportation" became increasingly muted as Americans raced to put four wheels under their seats and a roof over their heads. The motorcycle carried Jones to the fun. In this equation the motorcycle was the means; something else was the end. The equation had to be recast; motorcycling itself had to become the end.

No one had to spell this out on Juneau Avenue in Milwaukee. The founding fathers of Harley-Davidson realized that for fifteen years they had nurtured a sport while selling inexpensive transportation. Their new factory-to-rider publication, *The Harley-Davidson Enthusiast*, underscored that realization. In America at least, motorcycles would compete with swimming holes, not cars.

If the fun was getting there, then riders still had to have somewhere to go. No wonder then that the pages of *The Enthusiast* bulged with travel stories. The long roll—the ride that clocked mileage in borders crossed and famous places seen—was a standard dream for those who were just discovering what personal mobility inside a vast continent might mean. Of course there were railroads, but railroad tracks ignored a million places in America. Of course there were automobiles, but motorcycle enthusiasts loved motorcycles. So that exciting, tan-

When the day is over—when the busy week is spent—let no well earned opportunity pass by to refresh your mind and body.

Everyone needs recreation, and the Harley-Davidson will take you to the places where you want to go—will make it possible for you to enjoy events now beyond your reach.

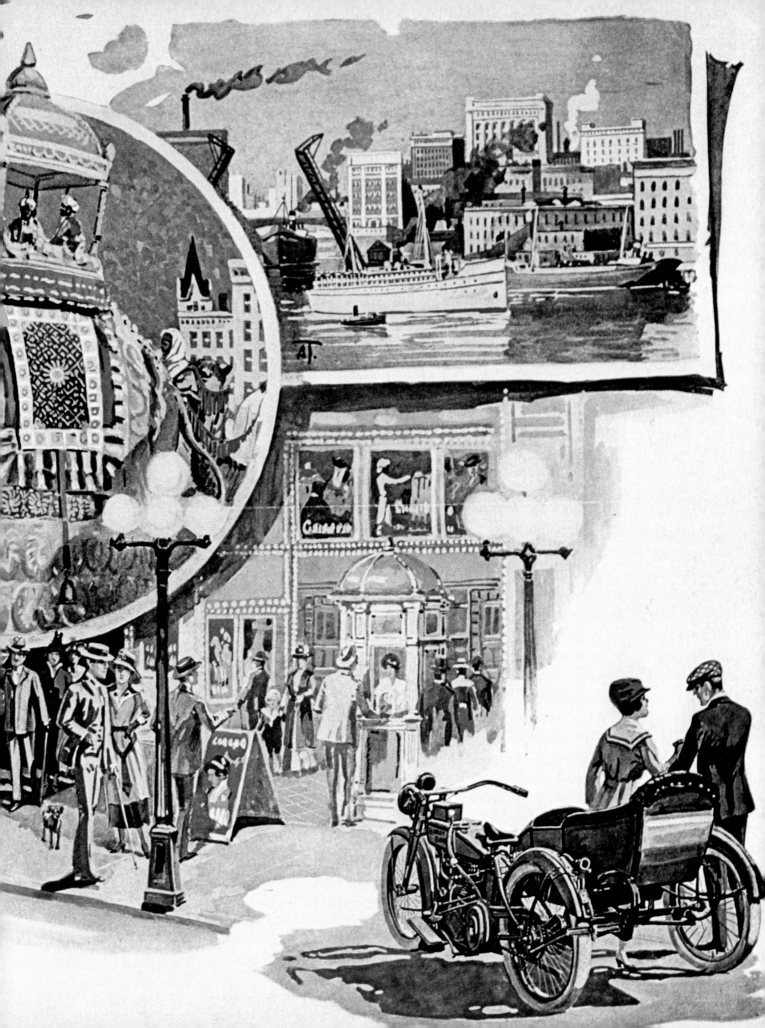

48

Kerle and Gerberick were just traveling men, roaming without a schedule. So their journey was far different from Cannonball Baker's transcontinental shot seven years earlier. With no clock and an uncertain route, the pair had time for camping, posing, clowning, and meeting other wayfaring cyclists.

talizing possibility lurked in the back reaches of every motorcyclist's mind: a long, rambling motorcycle roll, seeing a country unfold from a highway map. Breaking the bars no longer involved riding to the county fair. There developed a grander conception of imprisonment and freedom, and only crossing the far horizon would breach the bars and set the rider free. Motorcycling was sport and travel and liberation, packed together.

"We cared not how many miles we could make in a day," Roy Kerle wrote in 1922, recalling such a trip with Royal Gerberick, a western swing that began in Topeka, Kansas, on July 27, 1921, and ended there, a year and one hour later. Gerberick's 1920 Harley-Davidson 20J sidecar outfit hauled the two motorcyclists and all their gear: "A 7 x 7 tent with 3 ft. wall; 1 doz. iron stakes; two 7 ft. poles (jointed) and ropes; 4 army blankets; 2 army cots; folding grate; folding skillet; folding water bucket; 2 canteens; 1 water bag; 2 mess kits, cups, knives, forks, spoons and can opener; compartment can for sugar, coffee, salt and pepper; 2 saddle bags; suitcase; cover for machine; raincoats, sweaters, mackinaws and coveralls; bag for towels and toilet articles; army first-aid kit; camera and maps; hand axe, blow-out patch, extra tire; 3 extra tubes and all necessary tools, including a small vulcanizing outfit and sidecar wrenches. The tent with stakes and ropes folded and strapped on the luggage carrier of the machine; saddlebags with cooking equipment strapped to sides of carrier; an extra brace clamped to sidecar frame between body and wheel when set out, carried the cots and tent poles.

"The suitcase fit snugly to the floor of the sidecar, and sweaters, raincoats, mackinaws, etc., lay on top of it. The folding grate was placed on the luggage carrier on back of the sidecar and the cover for the machine on top of the grate. Blankets were strapped in the extra tire. The three extra tubes were folded and put inside of the extra casing which had a cover. The hand axe and all extra tools were placed under the sidecar seat. The toilet bag hung over the sidecar door, which was secured by straps fastened to the floor of the sidecar. The folding skillet, inside of the folding water bucket with the camera, fit in the nose of the sidecar. It is remarkable what one can put on a sidecar outfit without overloading."

With the Harley-Davidson 61-inch V-twin beating deliberately, the pair left Topeka on a heading that ran west through Dodge City, Kansas. At Green River, Utah, they wheeled northward, passing through Salt Lake City and Pocatello, Idaho. At Helena, Montana, they veered north and west, touching Spokane and Vantage before reaching Seattle, Washington. The route dropped southward, intersecting Portland in northern Oregon and Medford in the south. Their tracks went through Sacramento, California, before halting in Los Angeles where they stayed from October, 1921, to July, 1922. Then they struck east, across California, Arizona, New Mexico, the Texas panhandle, and Oklahoma. By the time they reached Tulsa, the Harley-Davidson was already pointed northward again, bearing toward Topeka and home. Mileage, including their side trips, totaled 19,000 miles.

Motorcyclists invariably write trip-diaries of weather and road conditions because, unlike other long-distance vehicles, the motorcycle's traveling environment is the sky above and the road below. Kerle and Gerberick uncovered roads in all conditions. Sometimes, Kerle noted, "roads" tagged along railroad beds. ". . . we started out to cross the hot sand and rough roads on our way to Green River, Utah, following an old abandoned railroad where, at times, we drove on what was left of road bed. Bumping over ties and crossing washes, back upon the road bed and then down again, we managed to get to the state line mostly in low and second. I mentioned that some day people would be going 50 miles per hour through this

The 1928 Henderson Four had
not yet been streamlined. The tank
still lived inside the frame
members instead of saddling the tubes.
The huge speedometer gearing at
the rear wheel connected openly with
the instrument. With cast-iron
heads and cylinders stacked four deep,
the engine was massive.

stretch. My partner said: 'Just lie there in the sidecar and keep on dreaming.' "

The Topeka pair had first-hand experience with that conspiracy between earth and sky called rain and mud. "I was always under the impression that it never rained in the desert. I've never seen it rain so hard. We were stranded and stuck tight in desert gumbo seven miles from town. With no sign of a break in the storm, we sat under the cover of the machine and waited. It was two hours later and getting dark before the rain stopped. We crawled out from under our shelter and looked around. Then we heard a car coming. It was a Chevrolet 490 and it sounded like it was going about 50 but it was hardly moving, slipping and sliding even with chains on all four wheels, and zig-zagging down what was left of the trail. When it stopped and the driver asked if we wanted a lift into town, we hesitated not. I think we made about a mile when we came to a small muddy wash. Stuck was no name

for it. My partner decided to hike into town along the railroad tracks while I spent the night in the back seat of the car with the four other occupants."

The devilish roads, Kerle observed, could snare cars but still allow the Harley-Davidson to chug off scot-free. In part anyway, the motorcycle paid back in power for its lack of a roof. And Kerle and Gerberick, bonded to the machine by adventure and adversity, looked at automobiles with traces of contempt.

"Many people . . . told us that we could not make it over Priests Pass (some called it Lookout Pass). It went in one ear and out the other; we let them do the worrying, not us. Now we were ready to tackle that 'awful hill.' This is where they get out and push the Fords over, most of them backing up to get gas to the carburetor. We went to the top in second, almost as if it was nothing to speak of."

Other places weren't so easy. "Then we . . . started up the Bitterroot Pass of the Camel's Hump. The

sign at the side of the road said: 'Fords, do your damnedest.' It was a real climb all the way to the summit. On the way we met a man with a team of horses. He had been helping pull cars over the last half-mile to the top all summer. It took all we had in low gear to make it."

The 1920 motorcycle endured. In Oakland, California, the valves were ground and the engine decarbonized. When Kerle and Gerberick reached Los Angeles, they concluded that they had made good time, considering that hurry had not been their purpose, and that they had encountered so many ghastly roads. Kerle summed the problems: "Two broken control wires, a stuck exhaust valve, three punctures (still had the original air in the front tire), one blow-out, and a broken mudguard brace." They had bought a tire on the way, replacing one which had been scuffed down to nothing when mud had caked up under the rear fender. Despite road conditions, Kerle and Gerberick had only minimal difficulties.

Homeward bound, after months of sightseeing in California and environs, Kerle surveyed the Southern California desert. "A junk man could make a good living (if not a small fortune) just by going along this route and picking up all the old tires, tubes, and automobile parts lying along the side of the road. But we were enjoying the ride and the country when what happened but a broken rear chain. The problem with all that sand was finding it. We got down and sifted about a block of sand before I finally stepped on it (having taken off my shoes earlier)."

In Arizona the road brutalized the motorcycle and sidecar. "I believe it is the most nerve-wracking road this side of hell . . . we crept along at 15 miles per hour." Even so, the sidecar frame fractured, but was shortly repaired. The experience left Kerle skeptical of New Mexico roads. "At Clovis we left New Mexico, a state where residents would faint if they saw a stretch of concrete road 10 miles long." Oklahoma wasn't much better. "East of Oklahoma City is a road called the 'Air Line' and about the only way this highway can be conquered is by air. We were in the air most of the time, bouncing and fighting the weeds grown high on both sides. Once we ended up in a corn patch on a detour."

Back in Topeka, "nearly broke, dirty, tired, but still enthusiastic," Kerle reflected upon all the miles, the roads, the bumps, and the future. "Maybe," he thought, in years to come "all those same roads will be paved. But that, I suppose, is just a dream."

Fewer heads than ever dreamed the dream of a long-distance roll. American motorcycling was deep in its winter of despair. The number of completed motorcycles decreased from about 60,000 in 1919 to 26,000 in 1921, and the number of motorcycle manufacturing companies dropped from twenty in 1919 to thirteen in 1922, while automobile makers proliferated.

Motorcycle spokesmen fretted. Motorcycling, it seemed, had shrunk to a minority composed of young enthusiasts whose high spirits and behavior—when connected to visible, high-performance machinery—could produce occasional results as inconspicuous as a fire bell ringing in the night. Suddenly motorcycling had an image problem. In his magazine, *Motorcycle and Bicycle Illustrated*, W. H. Parsons worried in print. If it had once been cheap transportation, motorcycling had become expensive entertainment. Because it was expensive, he argued, motorcycling was a "gentleman's sport."

Parsons' logic turned strange corners. Expense didn't make motorcycling an elite sport. Its "exclusivity" only served to make motorcyclists a minority group of motorists, and this minority had a troublesome subgroup of its own. Parsons was upset by that minority within the minority. "We who ride them and who consider motorcycle riding the greatest sport on earth have been careless of our appearance and our conduct. Some of us have acted like roughnecks and hoodlums. We have raced along the roads in grease-smeared clothing, with dirty faces and with open mufflers. We have made nuisances of ourselves and created a public prejudice that has resulted in making it unpleasant for the great majority who have conducted themselves like gentlemen. The number of roughneck riders as compared to the total is small, but it's the noisy ones who are noticed and it is by their conduct that we are judged as a class."

Later, Parsons concluded that motorcycling's future was pinned to "young unmarried lads," age eighteen to twenty-five. It was a sport for young working men. "We also hear much about selling to middle-aged white-collar prospects. A good many motorcycles have been sold and will continue to be sold to these prospects. Get all the professors, doctors . . . you can . . . but they will only be the froth on the top of the glass.

"The real stuff underneath, the foundation upon which the prosperity of industry must stand, will be the lads who ride from the fun of it and who must pay for their fun by the sweat of their brows."

The general public cared little for sociology. The public didn't know and didn't care that some motorcyclists' behavior might correlate to factors other than machinery. Most motorists "knew" that motorcycles flew down the highways, bellowed from exhaust pipes, and were dangerous, *prima facie*. Common sense—and the wisdom of majority numbers—sided with automobiles. Motorcycles were dumb transportation; cars were up the transportation ladder from motorcycles, so motorcycles must be low-brow. Motorcycles as sport vehicles? Indeed not, the knowing majority replied, sport is one thing but self-abuse quite another. In practical America, what could be more absurd than owning a frivolous, dangerous vehicle? Danger was the greatest impracticality of all. In the nineteen-twenties, Americans loved heroes and danger large

and abstract. Charles Lindbergh was perfect. But close to home, everyone was racing forward to get rich, to prosper, to enjoy more things. A better car fit the New Prosperity, and so did tube radios, and second bathtubs. Stark motorcycles didn't fit—no matter if princes rode them.

Police did ride them. Crime, reasoned one writer, was big business. "Whatever may be said for or against the automobile, it is the greatest accessory to crime the world has every invented. All first-class, high-grade criminals now operate *á la* automobile. . . . The best method yet invented [for catching automobile-equipped criminals] is the motorcycle. This is the one big opening and increasing field for the motorcycle. Crime is increasing at an encouraging rate, from a motorcycle standpoint."

Factory-to-rider publications paid tribute to this business in print and photograph. The police market was big and important. *Indian News* published a regular police feature, "Heroic Deeds By Motorcycle Officers," which carried stories like the following.

"At about 11:30 P.M. Officer Gennerich, while patrolling his post, observed an automobile going south on First Avenue [in New York City], at a high rate of speed. He started in pursuit. At 50th Street he timed the auto and found it to be going at better than 50 miles per hour. He opened the throttle of his Indian, came alongside the car and ordered the driver to pull over to the curb and stop. Instead of obeying, the car was driven forward at a greater rate of speed down First Avenue to 25th St., West to Second Avenue, South to 23rd St., where one of the occupants, Arthur Leslie, opened fire on Gennerich, from the back seat of the car, with a pistol which had a silencer attached. The officer had been the target for ten shots but was not aware of the fact until the bandit opened fire with another gun, which had no silencer. When Gennerich saw the burst of flame and heard the reports, he drew his pistol and fired three times, traveling at this terrific speed. One bullet penetrated the rear [brake] shoe [of the car] which caused it to swerve and come to a stop upon the sidewalk.

"When the crash came, Leslie, who had been firing at Gennerich, jumped from the car and made his escape but was captured later.

"Through the arrest of the driver of the car . . . and . . . his companion, it subsequently developed that the prisoners were members of the notorious band of criminals known as the 'Cowboy Gang,' whose criminal activities ranged from homicide to hold-up and various other classes of crime. . . .

"The round-up of this desperate band has been hailed as the greatest police achievement since 1895 when the 'Fire Bug Gang' was broken up."

If sheer speed counted for anything, the four-cylinder in-line Henderson Deluxe motorcycle might have had a lock on the two-wheeled law enforcement trade. The Henderson four was the product of the Excelsior Motor and Manufacturing Company, makers of the Excelsior motorcycles, which in the early nineteen-twenties were 61-inch V-twins built in the classic American form. The centerpiece of the Chicago company, owned by Ignaz Schwinn, the bicycle magnate, was the Henderson Deluxe. In demonstrations to police officials, Henderson uncorked its big four for a 98-mph pass in Chicago. Later in San Diego, the bike shot past police officials at 100 mph. Clearly the machine had power to humble almost any "criminal" car.

Nor was Schwinn simply interested in blitzing his way into the police business alone. He wanted to electrify all riders, so the four-banger turned record-snatcher. Wells Bennett, a professional racer and long-distance rider, single-handedly took a Henderson Deluxe to a twenty-four-hour closed-course record on the Tacoma (Washington) Board Speedway, a rough and splinter-infested two-mile track. The tires picked up splinters, throwing them in all directions. At times Bennett approached collapse. About ninety-five miles from the end, a crisis developed. "Stopped for rest. Bennett was clear gone. Going to sleep in the saddle. The pit crew put his head under the cold water faucet and brought him around; time out 3 min. 55 sec." Bennett and the Henderson covered 1,562.5 miles in 23 hours, 59 minutes, for an average of 65 miles per hour. The year was 1922. Schwinn got his record.

Later that same year Bennett chased Cannonball Baker across the continent. Baker started first, riding an Ace four-cylinder motorcycle which resembled the Henderson machine, and for good reason. Both had been designed by William Henderson, who, after selling the Henderson concern to Schwinn, fell out with the bicycle-maker and moved to Philadelphia, where he founded the Ace Motor Company. The trans-American record dispute was a six-cornered contest: two revered riders, two strong-willed manufacturers, and two famous brand names.

Baker rushed from Los Angeles to New York in 6 days, 22 hours, and 52 minutes. The day that Baker arrived in New York, Bennett, who had started out twenty-eight hours after Baker from Los Angeles, knew he could beat Baker's fresh record. But the Henderson rider, delayed by a series of problems early in his run, flickered at the end of his endurance. He had made up lost time by riding without sleep. Outside Philadelphia, Bennett went out. His telegram explained: "Able to beat Baker an hour or more until 40 miles from Philadelphia, when we struck dense fog. Impossible to make 15 miles an hour through it, so couldn't beat Baker. Two hours sleep since Hutchinson, Kans., three days; too exhausted to ride farther unless for record." Baker kept the record.

Losing came unnaturally to both Schwinn and Bennett. In October, 1922, Bennett took another crack at Baker's record, and knocked it straightaway out of the books: 6 days, 15 hours, 13 minutes, which slashed 7 hours and 39 minutes off Baker's Ace record.

The Henderson Deluxe motorcycles were not only fast, but refined, sophisticated motorcycles. The multicylinder design produced a vibration-free engine, at least compared to the singles and V-twins of the period. Since the sidevalve four-cylinder engine displaced almost 80 cubic inches, making a stone-slow Henderson would have been difficult. Silence was as much a Henderson virtue as speed. By 1924 spiral bevel gears in the transmission replaced loud, straight-cut gears, and a cam silencer muffled valve noise. And the Chicago four had some elegant engineering inside. A mechanical oil pump drew oil out of the crankcase and pressure-fed the oil to the main bearings and, through the hollow crankshaft, to the connecting-rod bearings, and into the transmission. There was no oil tank —all the oil was carried in the bottom of the crankcase— and no hand oil pump. The rider's only responsibility in the lubrication department was to replenish the oil supply in the crankcase every 500 miles or so.

In a period when most motorcycles had cast-iron pistons, the Excelsior company made alloy pistons standard equipment on the 1924 Henderson Deluxe models. If one wanted cast-iron pistons, he could have them for "ordinary riding or commercial service." Cast-iron pistons, though they might crack if the engine were spun hard, were quiet, since they could be fitted quite closely to the cast-iron cylinders. On the other hand, alloy pistons required greater piston-to-wall clearances. Otherwise, the pistons would expand at a faster rate than the cylinders, and the engine would seize. But generous clearances meant that the pistons slapped and rattled when the engine was cold and warming up. That behavior was very un-Henderson-like.

Henderson's optional alloy pistons seemed a mixed blessing. In 1924 Henderson developed alloy pistons which had splits in the skirts allowing for piston expansion, which in turn permitted a tighter cold fit inside the cast-iron cylinders. "In operation," Henderson claimed, "the split-skirt piston gives all the advantages of the alloy —viz: lightness, freedom from vibration, perfect cooling, higher speed, and quicker getaway. . . ."

Refined though it was, the Henderson, like the other in-line fours of the early nineteen-twenties, was doomed. The American motorcycle market was still on a slider, and continued to slip until 1930. The esoteric machinery appealed to that constantly shrinking group of seasoned motorcycle enthusiasts. The fours, standing at the peak of a shrinking mountain, were crowded from below by improving V-twins. To compete, manufacturers chopped retail prices of the fours, at times below production costs. The Ace Motor Company plunged off the peak in 1924. The Cleveland four, already late when first introduced in 1925, followed in 1929. By the time the American stock market went to rubble in October/November, 1929, and the country staggered into 1930, only two four-cylinder American machines remained: Indian and Henderson. Indian had revived the Ace, first offering an Ace-Indian and later an Indian four engineered in Springfield. The fours couldn't support themselves alone. The Indian multi stood at the front of the Springfield ranks filled with successful V-twins. The Henderson wasn't so lucky.

Ignaz Schwinn was a tight-fisted, conservative businessman who lived and worked by dicta. One such rule was never to buy anything unless you had the actual cash to pay for it. Schwinn had immigrated to America in 1892, and spent almost forty years painstakingly assembling his two-wheeled empire. The American economic collapse shook him badly. Fearful that the motorcycle business might go into the red permanently, he acted swiftly in 1931. Less of a gambler in his seventy-first year than ever before, he called in his department heads and in one terse phrase killed both Excelsior and Henderson: "Boys, today we stop."

Only the Indian four survived for another decade, almost an anachronism in a land of V-twins.

4.

singles and v-twins

That it works is the most important thing about a mechanical device. Had motorcycles failed to work, or work very well, two-wheelers would have gone to dust with those early contraptions which flapped wings and hopped vigorously but did not fly. No shining formulas cast certain light inside the labyrinth of progress; designers bumped and nudged their way forward in the dark. Engineers first worried that engines would run, then continue to run, and run well. None of the pioneers concerned himself about the abstract subtleties of "handling." Rather, the manufacturer might puzzle over the reasons why frames broke or forks sheared off—or why a particular machine wobbled incoherently at certain speeds and duly thrashed the rider into the bushes.

After making the machine work, the object was to make it more efficient. Second- and third-generation motorcycles were less ponderous and crude than the first generation. If the manufacturer could produce a more powerful and reliable model at lower cost, then he was money ahead. The 1920 Indian Scout, for example, could equal the performance of the 1912 61-cu. in. Springfield V-twin. The smaller 37-cu. in. engine developed about 11 hp on a dynamometer, whereas the 1912 model returned approximately 7 hp. The 1920 V-twin had a gear-driven primary which transmitted the power from the engine shaft to the clutch and the three-speed gearbox, and the engine formed a unit power plant with the transmission. The regular 1912 Indian twin had a chain primary drive, bicycle-pedal starting, and "direct" gearing. The 1920 Scout was progress, indeed. It was also the harbinger of new, small V-twins from Excelsior in 1925 and Harley-Davidson in 1929. Though the 45-cu. in. Excelsior superseded its larger predecessor, the compact V-twins hardly banished the 61-cu. in. models which Harley-Davidson and Indian continued to refine and develop.

Stubbornness didn't keep those big twins rolling out the factory doors. Economic conditions supported the heavyweights. As American motorcycling fell into lean years in the 1920's, circumstances rewarded conservative choices, punished radical ones, and arrested innovative engineering. When Indian introduced its small Scout, Harley-Davidson was already offering a 42-cu. in. opposed twin, with cylinders lying lengthwise in the frame. This creative piece of engineering didn't sell, but the peppy familiar-looking Scout did. The opposed twin shortly disappeared. Its brief career served notice to manufacturers that bold experimentation might carry heavy penalties. As the market tightened through the twenties, no manufacturer could afford to make a costly error. The tooling expenses for brand-new, breakaway models were enormous compared to any returns which might come from a sluggish market. Good strategy called for gradual improvement of existing motorcycles, introduction of evolutionary machines on a follow-the-leader or meet-the-leader basis, or on the certainty that new departures wouldn't threaten profits.

One such departure was the appearance of new Harley-Davidson and Indian lightweight single-cylinder motorcycles, which the industry hoped would tap a latent transportation market and expand the ranks of genuine enthusiasts. Some careful thought preceded the offering of these lightweights. In the mid-twenties, the argument ran, manufacturers had to expand the marketplace because the experienced "road hounds" who demanded bigger and faster machines every year were galloping the makers in an ever-closing circle, which eventually would choke the sport to death. Lightweight machines would attract young blue-collar workers who might become enthusiasts if they could buy into motorcycling at a low level. The lightweights could also be sold to people who wanted inexpensive transportation. Sophistry aside, the singles never fulfilled the expectations of their advocates. Automobiles controlled the transportation pipeline, and enthusiasts wanted V-twins.

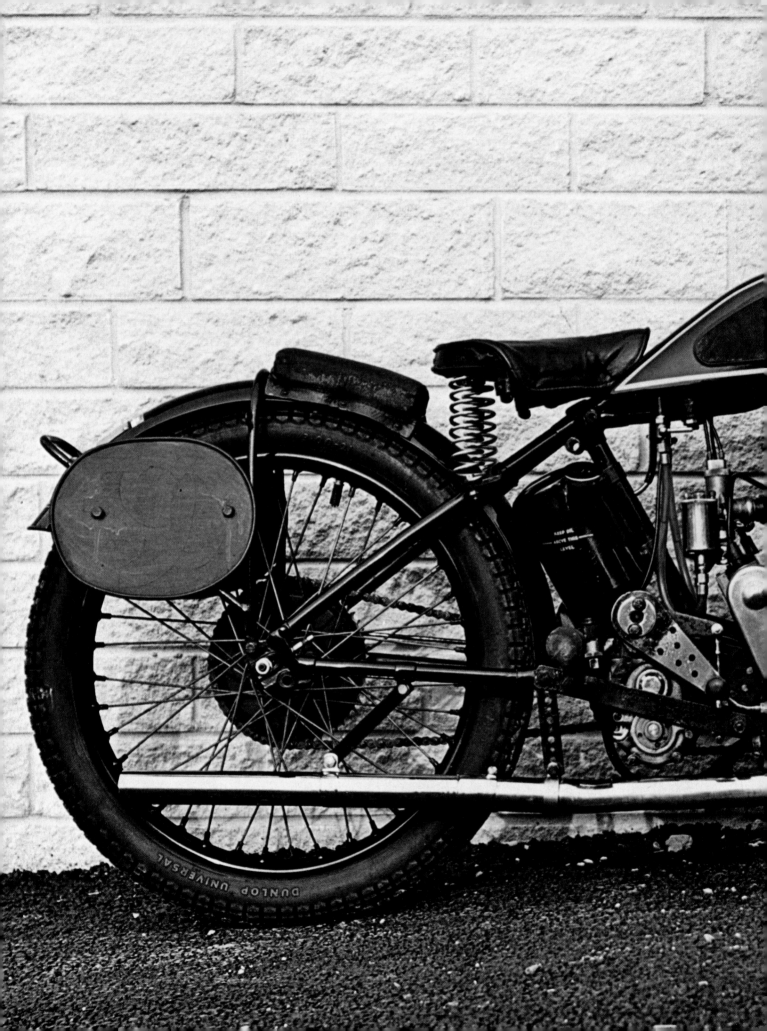

*Preceding pages: The immortal KTT
Velocette was a splendid example of the
creative conservatism in British
design. Right: Race victories begat
commercial success, and Velocette
traded on its racing reputation. Below:
The 1930 Junior TT at the Isle
of Man had riders of many nationalities
mounted on KTT racing machines.*

CARSSON
(WEDEN)

H.MITCHELL
(ENGLAND)

K.TADA
(JAPAN)

E.THOMAS
(ENGLAND)

D.HALL
(S.AFRICA)

H.J.WILLIS
(ENGLAND)

S.WILLIAMS RESERVE
(AUSTRALIA)

A.MITCHEL
(ENGLAND)

AURE
IN)

O. SEBESSEY
(HUNGARY)

J. HANSON
(ENGLAND)

S. SIK
(ENGL

A V-twin inertia prevailed. The configuration had been an accepted fixture in American design since the first decade of the century. Buyers responded affirmatively to machines in this pattern. Manufacturers, needing automatic acceptance in a low-volume market, were loath to stray far from orthodoxy. Seasoned riders preferred big twins, in part because Americans equated size with quality—the bigger, the better—and motorcyclists shared this cultural bias with everyone else.

The big V-twins were more than creatures preserved by market considerations and cultural preferences. They had other merits. V-twins ran more smoothly and evenly than single-cylinder motorcycles, though less so than a good four-cylinder bike. Since Americans wanted big engines, and a one-litre single would have been an engineering nightmare, anything less than a twin couldn't be considered. Given the cautious nature of decision-makers in Springfield and Milwaukee, the only other practical engineering alternative to a V-twin design was an in-line four. Even if cost had not been a significant factor, the in-line four seemed unlikely to break the V-twin hegemony. Unburdened by complexity, the V-twins as a group proved more reliable and fiddle-free than machines in the four-cylinder class. Furthermore, V-twin engines could be compact on the outside and carry big pistons inside. The narrow-angle V-twins fit naturally into motorcycle chassis, providing the largest displacement engines for whatever space was available.

Big pistons, and the big engines that went with them, had advantages that were apparent everywhere, from the factory machine-tool rooms to the highways. Any corporate bookkeeper could understand that manufacturing tolerances were greater when machining pistons 3½ inches in diameter than when cutting them to 1½ inches. Machining operations were less critical, quality control found fewer parts to reject, and productivity increased.

Big engines went into massive, husky motorcycles that could motor down long stretches of good highway at a fast clip without breaking, because those big pistons weren't working very hard.

Although Harley-Davidson and Indian pushed their 61-cu. in. engines of the 1920's to outer limits of 74 and 80 cu. in. respectively, their displacements hardly mushroomed like domestic automobiles. Contrary to popular assumption, American manufacturers did not gradually substitute cubic inches for engine technology. Big, simple, American V-twins started out that way and stayed that way. Conservative engineering adjustments produced substantial changes when applied to 74 cu. in. To the degree that those big, strong, slow-turning engines were inefficient, the giant V-twins stood convicted. "Workability" remained the American keynote.

Almost any single statement about the nature of British and European motorcycles and motorcycling can be nibbled away around the edges by exceptions. But there are some safe generalizations. First, motorcycles were both transportation and sport in England and Europe, but motorcyclist and enthusiast were not interchangeable terms. Second, British and European manufacturers sized engines and motorcycles smaller than did their American counterparts. Third, makers abroad turned out a variegated lot of motorcycles; no matter how bizarre or brilliant an idea, somewhere in England or Europe someone sometime tried to beat that idea into metal. However, those marvelous mechanical devices appeared only at the periphery of European motorcycling; simple single-cylinder machines constituted the hard core of motorcyles.

Point-of-view made the enthusiast. He who looked upon motorcycles as legitimate sporting vehicles qualified. In a world of perfect justice, all enthusiasts

66

Above left: This 1930 KSS was Velocette's standard high-performance roadster. Near left: A 1937 Mark II KSS bears strong resemblance to the earlier KSS. Above: John Goodman, founder of Veloce, Ltd., poses with Brooklands rider Rex Judd who is on board a mid-twenties Velocette utilitarian two-stroke.

would have owned proper sporting motorcycles. But injustice filled the world, so there was one group of sports made up of armchair or pillion-seat enthusiasts, while another class of boosters owned motorcycles that were only everyday dromedaries. Enthusiasts who rode the finest sporting motorcycles of the day constituted the upper class of motorcycling. And what did enthusiasts, for the most part, ride? Top to bottom, there was a standard idiom in machinery: the four-stroke, single-cylinder motorcycle.

Singles dominated a market which was active but not affluent. To those seeking transportation and/or sport, motorcycles were affordable, though usually not without sacrifice. A motorcycle was no frivolous purchase. It represented a substantial expenditure for which the buyer might well go into debt. The Great Depression consolidated the grip of the single-cylinder machine, as manufacturers struggled to broaden the utilitarian base of motorcycling. In England, for example, many manufacturers added cheap, basic, lightweights—propelled by Villiers proprietary engines.

Singles had fewer working parts and required less assembly time to produce. Like big American twins, singles had large working parts and gave good value. With one or two exceptions, it cost at least sixty dollars less to buy a single than a twin. The savings didn't end with the purchase. A good four-stroke single would perform well, and give long, reliable service while costing little to maintain. Excluding major tasks such as cylinder reboring, most repairs could be made in the garden shed.

Compared to a United States motorist, the European paid dearly for his gallon of gasoline, and governments soon found the taxation of private road-going vehicles a convenient way of raising revenue. To the extent that gasoline prices and taxation discouraged the construction and use of large vehicles, these factors spurred vehicle designs which squeezed great efficiency from a small as-

semblage of raw materials—ranging from aluminum to petroleum products. Not only did a European vehicle have to work, the thing had to be economical in terms of the resources consumed in building and operating it.

Efficiency, thus, had two aspects: economy and performance. The marketplace favored vehicles weighted toward economy, and therefore most motorcycles were economical transporters. Performance vehicles, built on the single-cylinder format, ran off in a different direction and extracted the most power and speed from an engine of a given size. For the sporting sector of the market, manufacturers could better spend their resources developing cylinder heads that would produce more power when bolted atop a single cylinder than tooling up for an engine with multiple cylinders.

Vehicles had to adapt to the British and European environment, which had been laid out and settled long before the age of powered vehicles. Narrow, winding roads in England and Europe throttled high cruising speeds. Neither the roads nor the total living environment encouraged large vehicles in general. Towns and villages punctuated British roads every few miles, and high population densities inhibited high speeds, as did the 20-mph limit which stayed on British books until 1929.

British and European manufacturers were less hidebound than American makers. Their marketplace had greater depth and variety than the American scene, and was not controlled by the single-cylinder in the way that America was by the V-twin. Competition among manufacturers produced innovative designs and accelerated technological developments. Much of this broad-ranging creativity came from small manufacturers, who could parlay a brilliant idea into a sales success, or innovate themselves right out of business. The general market wasn't shrinking, but the individual manufacturer was likely to be small and fragile and vulnerable to errors. Whoever operated outside

*The Indian company's long-lived
V-twin Scout series initiated the trend
to lighter, more compact
American twins. Indian began the
Scout line in 1920; pictured
opposite is the 1928 Scout. Many
Indian fanciers consider the
45-cu. in. Scout the best motorcycle
ever built by Indian.*

the standard single-cylinder idiom did so at considerable risk. Perhaps that delicate balance between old and new, success and failure, is what made the British such creative conservatives in motorcycling.

Even if economic conditions had dictated that only single-cylinder layouts were acceptable, from a manufacturer's viewpoint it was still not easy to divine the formula for a successful new design. Every company's board of directors wanted the near-impossible feat from its engineering department: Break new engineering ground, but don't gamble with company profits; design an engine so advanced that its production life might be measured in decades, but do nothing to startle and frighten off the initial set of potential customers. In 1923 exactly these sorts of demands faced Veloce Limited, a small British concern which produced Velocette motorcycles. Its successful two-stroke machines became dated with the appearance of practical four-stroke, overhead-valve engines. With both the intake and exhaust valves in cylinder heads with hemispherical combustion chambers, these overhead-valve engines demonstrated their technical superiority in terms of increased engine power. AJS motorcycles set the pattern, and soon every manufacturer, including Veloce Limited, went scrambling toward the four-stroke, overhead-valve, hemi-head, single-cylinder bandwagon.

Percy Goodman, eldest son of Veloce Limited's founder, John Goodman, had the task of designing a new engine. This model, the board of the company thought, should enhance the Velocette motorcycle's reputation for performance and reliability, providing quiet exhaust without undue power loss, maximum enclosures of working parts, and exceptionally good and reliable lubrication. That was a tough order for 1923, but then Percy himself had played a critical part in formulating the order. An individualist of unquestionable technical competence, he was allowed to go his own way.

When he had finished, Percy Goodman had designed the first practical overhead-camshaft motorcycle engine, displacing 348 cubic centimeters (21 cu. in.). The Goodman design leapfrogged ahead of the overhead-valve designs. The single overhead camshaft in the cylinder head was driven by means of bevel gears and a vertical shaft, so the need for pushrods to operate valves was eliminated. With camshaft, as well as valves, in the cylinder head, valve control was more positive and therefore engine speeds could be increased. Percy Goodman's engine illustrated the creative conservatism of British design. Working within the standard format (single-cylinder), he incorporated contemporary technology (overhead valves and hemispherical combustion chamber) and added his own innovation (workable overhead camshaft) to raise the efficiency of the standard and guarantee a long production life for his particular version of that standard design format.

Prototype engines had their problems, of course. In 1925, after some design changes, Velocette raced two machines in the Isle of Man Junior (350-cc) race, but both motorcycles dropped out with mechanical bothers. Velocette intended to try again in 1926, and reason endorsed another crack. The Isle of Man Tourist Trophy races, held in June every year, were the most prestigious racing events in the world. The Isle of Man, in the Irish Sea, contained a 37¾-mile circuit made up of public roads which were closed off for the races. The course, looping round the island's rough topography, strained riders and machines alike. Any deficiencies in roadholding, engine, brakes, or gearbox could not escape the demands of the long circuit. An outright win, like the Junior, underwrote the success of a new motorcycle, since British and European enthusiasts believed that truth was found in racing results. No wonder, then, that Veloce Limited sank almost every penny it had into winning the 1926 Junior race with their new overhead-camshaft model.

Alec Bennett, a rider of great talent, had already won the Senior race on two occasions when he approached Percy Goodman with perhaps the fairest proposition ever made in racing circles. Conscious of Veloce's financial corner, Bennett volunteered to become a member of the factory-entered team if he could ride one of the new overhead-camshaft models. If he won, as Bennett was convinced he would, he would take whatever was going in the way of prize money and bonuses from the accessory suppliers. If he did not, he would take nothing. Bennett's offer was a godsend for Veloce, since a rider of his caliber could virtually name his own terms. And Bennett made a fair deal for himself, too. He won the Junior race by more than *ten minutes* despite falling off on his last lap.

Bennett's win convinced enthusiasts that the overhead-camshaft Velocette had something special. As a result, orders for the road-going version flooded in. The win demonstrated for the first time the potential of the overhead-camshaft engine, a design which—until Percy Goodman's effort—had never been reliable enough to consider seriously. Veloce Limited launched their new motorcycle in glory, the basic engine triggering a phenomenally long production run of sporting KSS Velocettes. The origi-

nal overhead-cam design continued in production until the end of 1934, with only minor modifications aimed at boosting the power. In 1936 an updated version, the Mark II, appeared with a number of new features, such as light-alloy cylinder heads with fully enclosed valve gear, improved carburetion, and very handsome styling. Meanwhile, other manufacturers quickly originated their own overhead-cam designs, which became the sporting format.

Production of the KSS model finally ceased in 1948. Discounting the war years, the overhead-camshaft models ran on for seventeen years with the same basic design. The KSS Velocettes possessed those qualities for which the European enthusiast would pay a premium. The machine had a technical pedigree which traced in very short lines directly back to the Isle of Man, and victory. If the roadway was narrow and winding, so much the better for the KSS rider. The machine sliced around corners with authority and precision. The rigid-framed motorcycle would jar the rider who could not or would not avoid bumps, but sporting riders lived with some saddle-rattling because they knew that the chassis, which clutched the engine low in the frame members, could straighten corners with indifference.

Inset: Harley-Davidson followed Indian and Excelsior when it introduced a 45-cu. in. twin in 1929. Below: Far bigger news was the 1936 Harley-Davidson 61-cu. in. ohv V-twin. This big-incher testified to the strength of the V-twin concept and America's commitment to large motorcycles.

The hand-shift/foot-clutch system endured on American motorcycles; when a sidecar was attached, the system was convenient. Harley-Davidson's bullet headlamps, shown on a 1930 big twin, were briefly in style. Interest in transcontinental records remained high.

The fast man on a snaking road had no time to reach down and hand-pump an extra shot of oil to the engine. With the KSS that was never necessary because from the beginning the overhead-camshaft models had a dry-sump lubrication system. And the hard rider needed brakes. Brakes went on both ends of every KSS; the binders were drums with internal-expanding shoes. Roads which danced up and down from corner to corner taught the British early-on the value of a front-wheel brake for fast stopping.

The man in an exhilarating hurry wanted to stay in harmony with the saddle, bars, and pegs. The greatest economy in movement allowed him to commune with the machine. Reaching for a gearshift lever at the side of the tank was monkey-motion to a hard traveler. Velocette had the answer: By 1930 its clients could buy a positive-stop foot-operated gear-change on the KSS.

While European enthusiasts might race along from point to point, twisting a KSS engine to a giddy 5,000 rpm, and threading narrow roads which ran across the country in a string of nervous twitches, American enthusiasts rolled serenely atop the ever-straightening highways of the United States. In those days before World War II, the surfaces of American highways were hardened and smoothed out in packed dirt and gravel, asphalt and con-

crete. Where possible in a space-extensive country, Americans made the environment conform to the logic of motor vehicles, tunneling through mountains, cleaving hills, and leveling knolls. A winding road, Americans believed, was a relic of the nineteenth century. Better to have a straight road jumping over hills directly than a timid road creeping through the low spots and doubling back on its trail. The more efficient roads became, the less efficient—at least in terms of size and economy—American vehicles needed to be. But American machines had to be reliable at sustained high speeds in straight lines—which is exactly what big American motorcycles were.

The durability of KSS design had nothing on the basic Harley-Davidson big twin. That original inlet-over-exhaust-valve V-twin went into production in 1909 and was replaced in the 1930 model year. Of course, it wasn't the same machine in 1929 that it had been in 1909, but neither were the first and last KSS Velocettes. By European standards, American motorcycles made progress slowly. For example, it was 1928 before Harley-Davidson big twins sported front brakes. And that same year, though a throttle-controlled oil pump was fitted, the old V-twin still had total-loss oiling.

When Harley-Davidson retired the old twin, they sent out its successor. A new 74-cu. in., sidevalve engine,

which produced about twenty percent more horsepower than the old twin, rested in a new frame with new forks. Sidevalve engines, even in 1930, were hardly on the cutting edge of engine technology. Like its forerunner, this new twin had no recirculating lubrication system. Much was familiar to the eye: the "2-Bullet Headlights," the same sort of tank and fenders, the V-shape in the engine compartment. The 1930 Harley-Davidson V-twin, massive and strong, was an evolutionary machine—careful, circumspect, and almost plodding.

When the "revolution" came in America, Harley-Davidson announced it with a whisper. In 1936, Milwaukee quietly introduced an overhead-valve, 61-cu. in. V-twin, without fanfare or applause. Gradually, the company fed 2,000 of these motorcycles into the marketplace, testing owner reaction. The machine created a sensation. The valves were in the cylinder heads, the engine had a circulating oil system, and the hand pump was gone forever; the gearbox had four speeds; a new frame dropped the engine and center of gravity closer to the ground; the teardrop tank broke with traditional Harley-Davidson styling.

The British might have seen less freshness and merit in the motorcycle than Americans, but that didn't damp an English road tester's enthusiasm. *The Motor Cycle* (May 20, 1937) marveled at the power: "It is from 30 m.p.h. upwards that the Harley-Davidson becomes a real joy. Its acceleration is, without exaggeration, colossal. . . . In any ratio the terrific surge of power is breath-taking, particularly when accelerating from 20 m.p.h. to 50 m.p.h. . . . Just as the acceleration is remarkable up to 50 m.p.h., so it is above this speed, up to 80 m.p.h. and more." That kind of performance could be expected of the American twin. More surprising was the verdict on handling: superb at all speeds over good or bad surfaces. The cornering proved as amazing as the steering, which was beyond reproach. "The big machine can be swung round

bends at extraordinary angles, while bumps can be ignored." That was strong talk from enthusiasts who grew up on winding roads with good-handling singles.

A road tester could sense where the machine would deliver the most satisfaction. First the hint: "The comfort of the saddle has to be experienced to be believed. Adjustment is provided for the long coil spring in the seat pillar tube, and by this means a vertical movement of more than eight inches can be obtained." Then the point: "There is an indescribable thrill about riding this large machine along a wide, straight and deserted main road. Sitting bolt upright in armchair comfort, one can almost immediately command any speed up to 85 m.p.h. on the level." Harley-Davidson's new motorcycle had the American highway experience built into it.

When at last Harley-Davidson decided to shout about their new engine, they picked an appropriate American setting and mark. At Daytona Beach, Florida, they hauled out a special blue streamliner in an attempt to set the American straightaway record. On the long beach, Daytona's city engineer had plotted out a three-mile corridor which skirted the water's edge. Brightly colored flags marked the raceway. The middle mile was the critical distance, and bright red bunting flapped at each end of this all-important mile. Joe Petrali, a professional racer and a small, tough, fierce man, began his shakedown runs. First, mist and stiff north wind caused a delay. Later the streamlined machine tried to fly at 124 mph. The streamlining came off. Petrali took another shot, bagged the record, but wanted to try again. Once more the highly modified Harley-Davidson sped away, its deep-pitched drone breaking through the steady roar of the surf: 136.183 mph.

It was another new American record and a fitting one. In a land of vast space and open roads, a huge V-twin wrote its record in a dead-straight line. There wasn't a winding road in sight.

77

5.

EUROPEAN ORTHODOXY

Racing, as the word was spoken in British and European tongues, referred to one thing and one thing only: road racing. In America "racing" might attach itself to any number of prefixes in the sport and become dirt-track racing, speedway racing, motordrome racing. Racing was never a word with sharp edges and a singular meaning. This shouldn't suggest that Americans were fuzzy of mind, content to garble the language of motor sports. More than anything else, the European precision in the matter came as a natural consequence of the origins of racing in Europe.

Racing began—or tried to begin—on public roads because, with one or two exceptions, roadways offered the only place where speed contests could be held. Unlike the United States, Europe was not space-extensive, and Europeans would not squander space building places in which to race vehicles. If a suitable piece of road already existed, European motorcyclists were able to get a hearing, and perhaps a road closure. As a minority activity in the United States after World War I, motorcycling couldn't get that kind of treatment.

In Europe, stealing part of the road system for a racecourse, if only for a few hours during a weekend, was a solution of elegant simplicity. What could be more logical than racing machines on the very roads for which they were intended? To the European mind, the vehicles had to adapt to the environment, since no one was about to rearrange centuries-old cities, villages, and countrysides to conform to the logic of motor vehicles. To say that the motorized contraptions had to be adaptive was just another way of saying that motor vehicles had to be practical and fit the roads that webbed the countryside. No wonder, then, that when racecourses finally were built in private parks, they mimicked the old public roads. Thus did the Europeans preserve the practical connection between road racing and everyday motoring.

From the logic of that connection sprang the idea that "racing improves the breed," a phrase that makes sense only when racing machines and road models bear some resemblance to one another and are adapted to the same set of conditions. Motorcyclists believed that racing improved the breed at a time when road-racing machines and street motorcycles were cast from the same mold. But in the 1930's racing motorcycles irreversibly moved toward specialization, and as differences between models increased, the chances of consequent improvement in street machines diminished.

To "improve the breed," a factory raced a motorcycle similar to a common production model, flogging it until it revealed its weaknesses or broke. The racer was then beefed up or changed—increment by increment—until the breakage of a particular part stopped, or until ill behavior ceased or something else in the bike failed. This new knowledge was incorporated into the production-line motorcycles. The improving-the-breed method, then, was really a break-it-and-fix-it system. Factories and enthusiasts assumed that pieces which broke under racing stress would, with enough time, produce similar trouble in production-line machines.

As engineering knowledge about motorcycles and internal-combustion engines increased, designers were —or should have been—less dependent on trial-and-error methods. One could, technically at least, go from that knowledge to the blueprints to an errorless final product. Or nearly so. For racing purposes, a company might design racing machines which had little to do with the machines they built for general use on the street or trails. The pain of upgrading the racing machine remained, but the agony of improving the common breed piecemeal—by jumps, snags, and snitches—ended.

Racing on public roads was the only way to preserve the connection between racing and road machines and, indeed, the whole system of breed improvement. The

Opening pages: On the Isle of Man,
World Champion Giacomo Agostini
and his MV Agusta reach the bottom of
Bray Hill. Road racing belonged
to the British and Europeans. Yankee
models rarely finished well. Below:
Fred Dixon motored an
American-made Indian into third
place in the 1923 Senior TT.

81

French and Belgians started road racing motorcycles soon after the first viable, powered two-wheelers sputtered and chugged to life. Racing activity increased on the Continent, and by the early 1920's British and Europeans were racing motorcycles in a series of Grand Prix events in certain specific displacement classes: the 500-cc Junior, the 250-cc Lightweight, and the 175-cc Ultra-Lightweight. In 1938 a formal European Championship system replaced the informal championships of the mid-1930's. By the time the Fédération Internationale Motorcycliste had determined the rules, some playing fields had already been established, and the grandest theater of all was an island.

Of one thing the British government had been faithfully certain: Whatever foolishness the continentals might tolerate on public roads, no such indulgences would be permitted in England. Public roads were for public travel. Racing thereon was prohibited. This bureaucratic hardheadedness left the Auto-Cycle Club solidly parked with its plans for racing until, following the lead of the Royal Automobile Club, its members carried their problem to the Isle of Man, whose government warmed to the idea of holding motorcycle races similar to the races already supported there by the Royal Automobile Club. And like the automobile chases, the motorcycle events took the name of Tourist Trophy races, all of which suggested the close relationship between racing and touring. Indeed, the first TT contests were both races and economy runs, since some bright souls believed that a hobbled race struck the best balance between touring and racing. Single- and twin-cylinder motorcycles ran in separate races, with the twins getting slightly larger gasoline allotments. Beyond gasoline rationing, the riders faced real touring-type situations—that is, when the road graded upward, riders pedaled furiously (it was 1907) or, as a last resort, pushed.

Soon the Isle of Man event had become an institution, the most permanent fixture in motorcycle racing. The island test was the supreme example of the European orthodoxy, road racing. Long and difficult, the course de-

manded much from riders and machines, and forgave precious little. Some names around the circuit belonged to the island's long past. Those ancient Manxland points curled and tripped from the foreign visitor's tongue as unrecognizable lumps: Kerro Mooar, Ballagaraghan, Cronk ny Mona. Then there were the easy ones, such as Sulby Bridge, Union Mills, and Windy Corner. Motorcycle racing, which interlocked with the island's recent past, added names of its own: Birkin's Bend, the Guthrie Memorial, Handley's Cottage. The past was rich enough to endow almost every twitch in the road with a name, and a history—real, embellished, or something in between.

When the Auto-Cycle Club officials replotted the course in 1911, they had no idea what the future might bring for Tourist Trophy races. The 1911 reconstruction of the course moved the race out of the southern lowlands to include the highlands of the north, thus drawing the racing map close to its final pattern. Earlier the circuit had been pinned down in the south because the pedal-equipped, single-speed, belt-driven wheezers couldn't have cleared Snaefell Mountain without the help of blistered feet and hard breathing. As finally plotted in 1920, the course

snaked and weaved and jigged up and down for 37¾ miles.

"The TT," allowed Oscar Hedstrom, head of the Indian factory, "is the most terrific thing I ever saw." It should be remembered that Hedstrom offered this testimony before his motorcycles won the Tourist Trophy race in 1911, though the American victory no doubt confirmed the Yankee's belief. Indian, as Americans fondly remember, swept the TT in 1911 with their V-twins equipped with four-plate clutches, two-speed gearboxes, and all-chain drive. These machines had some engineering margin on the opposition, inspiring one American reporter to quack that the victory proved "the superiority of American mechanical genius over other nations." Jake De Rosier, the American champion, spearheaded the attack. (He was also something of a fashion plate; his riding gear included black dancing tights, track shoes, and a blue woolen cap—an outfit that went well with his red Indian. "A champion's prerogative, I presume," observed one bystander sourly.)

The roads of the circuit were part dirt, part stone. About three-quarters of the course was laid out in crushed stone and dirt, charitably referred to as macadam surfacing. The Americans would have routed the British

on the road had it not been for C. R. Collier. The Matchless rider finished in second place but lost it for taking on extra gasoline illegally. After officials booted out Collier, Indian motorcycles filled the first three places, a great triumph.

Even in 1911, roadside spectators, as well as race officials, had plenty to watch: "At Quarter Bridge, where there was the most dreaded turn, exciting scenes were taking place. Jones, considered an expert at taking turns, in taking this bad one, actually rode up the curb, struck the wall of the bridge with his foot rest, bounced back, and set off without stopping. . . . This corner was so dangerous that preparations had been made for the worst

kind of mishaps. Everything was in readiness, but luckily nothing serious happened. A clever piece of riding thrilled the spectators here. Applebee was riding in the clouds of dust sent up by Franklin's Indian down to the bridge. He was going at full speed, almost to the turn and here he bluffed Franklin and shot around the corner a length ahead, picking up wonderful speed on the stretch. Just then, Jake De Rosier tore past, riding in splendid form, and with a lead of 33 seconds over Collier."

De Rosier, motor racing's peacock, soon encountered less splendid moments. "Later it developed that Jake had fallen between two other riders and smashed his

foot rests and bars. He resumed riding shortly, and was received with a tremendous ovation all along the line because of his apparent pluck."

Even the race's new leader, O. C. Godfrey, had his moments: "Indians were now first, second, and fourth, and an Indian victory seemed assured. As Godfrey passed on his last lap, going at a tremendous clip, his machine swerved, and the spectators held their breaths for a second, a death-dealing smash seeming inevitable. He regained position, however, and passed on."

Godfrey approached the finish line about a lap later, having averaged 47.5 mph for 187.5 miles: "The figure was bent far down on the machine, his nose almost touching the tank, as he tore past the post, and wobbling as he reduced speed. It was Godfrey, sure, and he was the winner, but by seconds."

"*Motor Cycling*, published in London, says of the winner: 'How that little shrimp of a man could have held and steered that palpitating red American racer for that distance over those awful roads, at that speed, is a thing that passes men's understanding!' "

By 1967 the age of the awful roads belonged to the past, together with the red-tanked palpitaters. For those few Americans who fancied genuine road racing, the Isle of Man remained mecca. Few Yankees had ever seen the TT, but that hardly dimmed the island's glow, for the importance of an event can grow in direct proportion to its distance from the beholder. Viewed from afar, "The Island" shimmered in mystical splendor. No mere mortals raced there; giants did. Winning motorcycles were more than machines; they were legends. Races weren't races, they were god-like struggles.

John Covington came away from the Isle of Man's Diamond Jubilee and filed his report in the October, 1967, *Cycle* Magazine. To Covington's eye, the pavement appeared smooth when he drove a car around the course that year. The circuit was still ". . . laid out in roughly a rectangle that neatly skirts the mountains on three sides, until, as if finally having made up its mind, it soars upwards from sea-level at Ramsey nearly 1,400 feet on the shoulder of Snaefell before plunging back down to the finish line in Douglas. You make your first circuit in about an hour, seeing for the first time the famous course points echoed in legend. . . . Strange and suggestive names—you are disappointed when you first see the reality.

"That lesson could only come from about a dozen men of this earth, one of those who had had the courage and skill and a sufficiently quick motorcycle to lap the Island course at over 100 mph. Because on your own lap at 65 mph you are only impressed with the smoothness of the pavement and the very many flat-out straightaways, and the gentleness of most of the curves, and you conclude that it's only a stronger engine that gets the average to the ton [100 mph], that you could do it yourself given 80 bhp and a fair set of brakes. By the time you ask the Famous Man, who in our case was the former Yamaha works rider Mike Duff, you have already reached your conclusion, lost interest in the problem, and resolved to find out how this champion managed to out-con all the others.

"All of which is reversed very promptly as soon as the good Mr. Duff, who has just laid down the wrenches with which he has been reassembling his Aermacchi 350 and climbed behind the wheel of your sluggish BMC 1100, turns onto the course a quarter-mile from the start headed down Bray Hill and begins a patter that runs something like this: 'On the G-50 you reach about a hundred and forty in fourth down here, fast enough to leave the pavement twice, here . . . and here, before you shut off for the left-hander and Quarter Bridge, take it wide, between the manhole covers, but not out on the gravel or off-camber, then down on the tank, back up through the gears flat-out —by flat-out I mean accelerating as fast as you can. If you

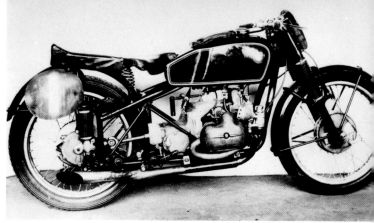

know the line, it's fourth gear all the way to Braddan Bridge; if you have a four-speed box, gear down here and here but don't lean it until you see the chimney on the second house, stay in the middle on the bridge, back to the curb, then wide enough to brush the Dunlop bag with your elbow....'

"And on and on, almost like a ten-track tape recorder that has itemized every pebble, bush, pole, building, shadow, grade, camber, and temperature change for 37.73 miles and is ready to revise or reiterate them instantly and without error. 'You know your G-50 is really on note if you leave the ground here.... Take these three left-handers in one sweep.... This one looks slow but take it wide open.... Here your biggest problem is wrestling the bars to keep the front end pointed down the road.'

"Meanwhile, the little 1100 is being thrashed within an inch of its life; you have turned ashen white; he crests a hill at 80 only to confront a herd of sheep in the road, slam to a halt, roar off again—two full-stop signs on the circuit—up over the mountain. Your head is reeling. Mike is talking calmly, hampered by the speed limitations of the car, and you remember someone saying the course has only one jump left, and even the 1100 has been airborne three times. You pull to a stop in front of his garage, your watch showing a lapse of a bit over thirty-two minutes, or an average of about 70 mph, and all the warning lights on the BMC are lit up like a Christmas tree and the engine sounds a little funny and Mike's father comes out and says, 'Good thing there's no toilet here; we have to go up to the pub,' and you all go up to the pub for a few pints and you mellow on how good it feels to be a Wiser Man."

The Isle of Man became motorcycling's very special place because those enthusiasts who go to the island in June feel a sense of participation, as if they are an integral part of race week, which of course they are. The apartness of the island and the time-scale of the races (one

week) confer that feeling of motorcycling's special place and time. All great racing events produce that sense of connection and participation, which is a far different thing than being entertained in a passive way by performers. What occurs on the Isle of Man is a rock-concert happening without music, a kind of motor concert. The sheer mass of mankind present produces a sense of importance on the part of all individuals who begin to feel a connection with the event at large. And that's something beyond spectating.

The British managed to keep a grip on Isle of Man Junior and Senior class racing until the years following World War II. But the competition in Grand Prix racing stiffened as the 1930's moved toward the second global conflict, and the British found themselves and their single-cylinder motorcycles pressed by the Germans and Italians, who were beginning to develop machinery that passed beyond the conventional boundaries of traditional single-cylinder designs. The British continued to refine the single-cylinder form. The Junior and Senior bikes raced by Norton and Velocette were fashioned in the classic mold.

In a way, the British may have been racing too intently for too long by the time they reached the mid-1930's. The fact that they had been Grand Prix racing longer and with more success than anyone else was their greatest strength and greatest weakness. In American parlance, the British were the most track-wise people in the business. More than any of their adversaries, they recognized the variables that made the difference between winning and losing in a particular contest—variables which included the horsepower available at the rear wheel, the way a racer's clothing fit him, the possible changes that alternative damping might make in high-speed handling, the care with which tire tubes went into the tires. That detailed view of the racing world, from which so many victories came, tended to blur the larger picture—the fundamental need for a new generation of racing equipment.

The British saw "all-new," "world-beating" engines from foreign makers enter long periods of development difficulties, then never quite deliver on their promise. The British vision of the development process encouraged creative conservatives to stay conservative, to keep winning while new-generation motorcycles broke. What was true of new foreign designs also applied to the most daring British departures. The AJS V-4, which sprang star-crossed from its mold in the mid-1930's, was a breakaway piece of engineering. Before AJS was finished, the factory had built new frames and different brakes, then supercharged and water-cooled the overhead-camshaft, four-cylinder machine, and—after all the trouble—the motorcycle was still not a winner.

The British had stayed with refinement and development for so long that their new machinery reverted to the break-it-and-fix-it tradition. Revolutionary machinery that came off British drawing boards had endless teething problems. The old break-it-and-fix-it routine had worked with singles, but the more complex motorcycles required a yet more complicated and baffling fix-it system. Soldiering through disappointment might have been easier for the British had not their single-cylinder racers been so successful in their own right.

Until the late 1930's the British had been able to increase the power of their singles sufficiently to keep pace with their continental rivals. Since they were track-wise enough to build a balanced machine—usable power packaged with good handling, braking, and reliability—they had no need to win a horsepower race. But they had to stay near. Norton, for example, moved from a single-overhead-camshaft cylinder head to a new double-overhead-camshaft head. In an effort to raise crankshaft speeds and thus power, the factory cut the stroke dimensions on the 350 and 500 works machines. Brakes became larger and lighter. Rigid frames made way for plunger frames. Ve-

locette followed a similar pattern, introducing the modern swinging-arm frame, which controlled up-and-down rear-wheel movement first by means of air-oil shock absorbers, and later by coil springs and oil damper units.

But no matter how creative British makers might be, they were caught in the vise of two laws: the law of diminishing returns combined with that of increasing difficulty. Together these laws doomed the British single. After the British bikes reached the shortened-stroke, double-overhead-camshaft level, every additional horsepower became really difficult to get. There wasn't another ready progression, such as a triple-cam desmodromic cylinder head, within reach. There was nothing that could produce a substantial jump in horsepower just by being bolted atop the cylinder and piston. Veloce, for one, was looking for that next big innovation which could be adapted directly to their single. That search explains the work on a rotary-valve cylinder head. Had that experiment proved successful and raised power output drastically, the new cylinder head would have greatly prolonged the life of Velocette single-cylinder racers. However, the rotary-valve induction system opened a snake pit of engineering problems which Veloce could not overcome. So the company gave up on the experiment and began work on a more conventional route to more horsepower—a supercharged engine.

The law of diminishing returns dictated that every additional horsepower did less than the one before. Getting a machine to 125 mph from 100 mph required far more horsepower than raising the speed from 75 to 100. Such considerations were academic for the 1940 season. World War II began and all racing ceased.

Postwar, the FIM banned supercharging and decreed that low-octane "pool" gasoline should fill the tanks of racing machines. These rule changes, the FIM believed, would encourage participation by manufacturers who were busy rebuilding factories and had few resources

Near right: Moto Guzzi won the 1957 350 World Championship with their streamlined single. Far right: Dustbin fairings, outlawed in 1958, were replaced by dolphin-types, shown on a 250 Honda four. Bottom: John Surtees howls the MV Agusta four, with a half-fairing, around the Isle in the 1956 Senior.

with which to continue the complex supercharged prewar designs. That was welcome news for the British, because their competitive prewar machines had not been supercharged anyway. They could lower their compression ratios to run on pool gasoline and go racing successfully with the same old singles.

In two years' time, more sophisticated designs again hounded the British singles, and again the British responded. Norton, for example, introduced in 1950 the "Featherbed" racing frame with swinging-arm rear suspension. Used with Norton's proven "Roadholder" telescopic forks, the machine set a standard for handling. Later, Norton lightened the factory machines, twice rearranged the bore-and-stroke dimensions, shortening the stroke and raising the redline and the power. But by 1955 the British were sitting out the series. Unless they developed specialized racers, they were simply outclassed.

Though the FIM had renamed the European Championships after World War II, the new label, World Championships, seemed a bit incongruous. For that matter, there was no participation by the United States, where there had never been any real interest in road racing. Also, the increasing use of highly specialized, not-for-sale, exotic racing machines in European road racing ran counter to American thinking. In the United States, the era of special racers had passed, and Americans believed in racing modified road machines. In a curious way, that was Norton's complaint in 1955 as it moved to the sidelines. To compete further, the company would have to build exotic one-off specials, which could contribute nothing to their street machines or their producton racers. Norton officials had no interest in such specials.

The German approach to Grand Prix road racing was different from that of the British, and proceeded in a rather abstract way. Building one-off specials didn't deter the Germans. They welcomed a playing field with a minimum of rules. The Germans produced machines which seemed unnecessarily and even strangely complex. The engines could almost appear to be design-room exercises rather than real racing-motorcycle engines with which mechanics and riders would have to cope at a racetrack. The prewar 250 DKW—supercharged and water-cooled— was a marvelous piece of machinery, somewhat akin to a mousetrap with a system of bellcranks, heim joints, rods, and levers which would dispatch the rodent by dropping a brick on it from an altitude of ten feet. German exercises, like the DKW, could leave an observer with two distinct reactions: Incredible! and Why?

Had the Grand Prix contests of the late 1930's been held on a dynamometer, rather than on racecourses, the Germans would have fared even better than they did in the prewar period, which was very well, indeed. The Germans appeared in force on the Grand Prix scene much later than the British; their start from clean sheets of drawing paper lent a kind of abstractness to their approach. For these relative latecomers, the best and fastest way to produce results hinged on building very special and powerful engines. Sheer horsepower could be a shortcut to the winner's circle and might overcome a multitude of other sins, among them excessive weight and high fuel consumption.

The maturation of the German crash programs brought forth some highly specialized racing hardware. Their racing-motorcycle design branched away from common road motorcycles. Though the Germans, like the English and Italians, did offer production racing models to private entrants, these commercial racers, produced in limited numbers by the factories, were in most cases more closely related to sports road machines than to the actual machines put into the racing field. More clearly than others, the Germans were no longer racing to improve the breed, because their street motorcycles and factory Grand

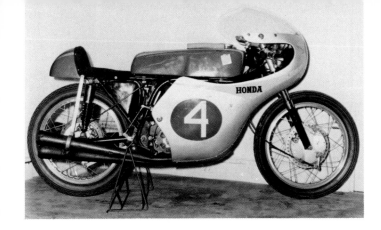

Prix racers had always been quite different horses.

The Germans were determined to prove they could master the Grand Prix racing game. Racing leadership seemed only a natural extension of the German lead in world motorcycle production. By the mid-1930's, German motorcycle production dwarfed the output of all other countries. In 1936, for example, Germany produced 151,195 of the world's total production of 316,810 units. By comparison, second-ranked Great Britain accounted for 75,300 machines, while the United States trailed far behind with 17,380. Such statistics suggest the strength of the base from which the Germans operated their racing programs. The German production figures reflected a returning prosperity. All those little motorbikes with their teacup engines, as well as the larger models, were phased to a general transportation market which, in turn, followed a prospering general economy.

Whether one considers the 500-cc, supercharged, opposed-twin BMW, or the supercharged, water-cooled, rotary-valve 250 and 350 DKW's, or the twin-cylinder, double-overhead-camshaft NSU 350 and 500 racers, one compelling fact stands out: The Germans tied their hopes of winning to outpowering their adversaries. That trick wasn't a new one. Mercedes-Benz and Auto Union played the same number in automobile racing, but the power-up play worked less well with motorcycles than with automobiles. Bolting a powerful engine into a motorcycle resulted in an ill-handling beast. Consequently, the

Near right: Giacomo Agostini angles off into Governor's Bridge on the Isle of Man during the 1970 Senior TT. Far right: The real "hump" bridge on the course is Ballaugh Bridge which is taken in first gear. The racing line goes airborne momentarily and then swings near the right-hand curb.

battles of the late 1930's pitted British handling and reliability against German horsepower and fragility. Once the Germans pieced their reliability factor together and found riders who could wrestle the bikes around fast circuits, the Germans dominated the faster tracks, while the British held the handling courses. The 1939 battle for the 350 Junior title was typical. The DKW's could overpower the slower Velocettes, but they fell victim to British handling on tighter, more demanding road courses. That stand-off created a tight-wire contest. It was touch and go all season, but Velocette brought the championship back to England.

The Germans, for all their problems with handling, were on the cutting edge of development. No one else had ever tried to shoehorn so much power into two-wheelers. If official figures can be trusted, the 500-cc NSU delivered 90 hp, and the BMW 500 racer 78 hp. Thus, the BMW's had nearly 30 hp and 20 mph in top speed over the Norton single. And after the BMW went through a weight-saving drill, the BMW 500 emerged weighing twenty-five pounds less than the Norton. The British knew how to make proper steerers out of their machines, and there was always a smug conviction that someone—English, of course—could have made the German juggernauts behave on the road. Had the British had as much horsepower as the Germans, their handling would have gone ragged, too. Though they tagged behind the British, the Germans weren't exactly laggards in frame technology. Their problems were monumental because their horsepower simply outran the ability of frame technology to contain it. Nevertheless, that was the trade-off the Germans had picked in an effort to produce quick results.

DKW took the European honors for 250 Light-weights from 1935 through 1939. BMW snatched the Senior crown in 1938. And NSU, which started its full-tilt Grand Prix program late, came up empty-handed before World War II, but collected five World Championships for Germany after the conflict.

The Italian way to Grand Prix racing was a divided path. Gilera, for example, displayed almost Teutonic directness with development of its supercharged, water-cooled, transverse, four-cylinder racer, which won the 1939 500 title. Other smaller concerns took the British approach, refining and honing a basic single-cylinder design. At their best, the Italians seemed to achieve a blend of horsepower and roadholding that marked them as track-wise competitors with an openness toward experimentation and the will to do it. Moto Guzzi's racing program best represented the Italian way of doing things. The Guzzi concern appeared on the international scene in the late 1920's but stayed at the periphery until its 120-degree V-twin won the Isle of Man in 1935. It was the first time an "outsider" had won the island's Senior event since the Indian sweep in 1911, and the Guzzi forecast a later continental onslaught on the island. The Italian 500 had a spring-controlled, pivoted-fork rear suspension. Moto Guzzi was the news story of the 1935 island events. A Guzzi springer also won the 250 race. The Guzzi victories were the first springer wins on the island.

The Guzzi was a middleground sort of machine. The overhead-cam V-twin had more potential than the British singles, but the Italian bike wasn't in fact faster or more powerful than the British. Any technical superiority the spring frame held over the rigid-frame machines more than disappeared when the British machines developed plunger frames and genuine swinging-arm frames a year or two later. In truth, the Guzzi V-twin was one of those machines which might have been a better performer than Nortons or Velocettes but which really didn't produce what its technical papers seemed to promise. In any event, Moto Guzzi found itself in the same sinking boat with the British in the late 1930's. Both were outpowered by the supercharged Germans and the Gilera. Guzzi, like Velo-

cette, built a supercharged 500 just before World War II intervened and halted racing.

After the war, Moto Guzzi again found itself in company with the British. Norton and Velocette ran singles in the 500 and 350 classes. Guzzi's new horizontal, single-cylinder, overhead-cam 250's put together a string of World Championships in the Lightweight class: 1949, 1951, and 1952. The Italians, as well as other continentals, showed more interest in the small-displacement class than did the British. The preference mirrored home markets. In Europe during the postwar period, tight-belted consumers considered a 250 or 350 a big bike. Since consumers were buying basic transportation, they shopped for reliability, durability, and a certain level of performance. If a 125-cc model, or even a 50-cc tiddler, met those needs, then no good reason existed for buying anything larger. One didn't go off and buy an expensive 500-cc motorcycle in postwar Germany without careful consideration, even if one could afford the tax and operating costs. The upshot of European buying trends was the concentration of Italian and German manufacturers on small-displacement motorcycles. The FIM recognized the importance of smaller motorcycles when it established a 125-cc World Championship in 1949. (The 75-cc class had died in the 1930's.) And firms like Moto Guzzi naturally concentrated first on small racing motorcycles.

For Moto Guzzi, starting with lightweight machinery meant that it was able to keep its singles competitive longer than the British, because the Italian singles—350's and 500's—were grown-up lightweights. Fergus Anderson, a factory rider for Moto Guzzi, convinced the company to enlarge one of the very successful 250 singles into a 350. At the time, that was a fairly inventive thing to try, as most 350's were 500-cc Senior bikes with engines 150-cc smaller. Guzzi thus discovered a formula for further development of the single. It found the next stage of refinement for singles: light weight, good handling, and fantastic streamlining. The first Guzzi 350 single touched the scales at 264 pounds in 1953, and although the engine developed only 31 hp, the full dustbin streamlining split the air neatly for 130 mph. By the time Moto Guzzi had finished building on this development, it had created a 350 Junor bike which weighed 216 pounds, droned out 38 hp, and ran 145 mph. Despite the competition of four-cylinder 350's, the fleet little Guzzi won the 1957 350 World Championship. Craft could still whip horsepower.

Unlike the British, the Guzzi firm could see the blackness at the end of the single-cylinder tunnel, and it had the wherewithal to start digging in another direction. First, it built an in-line, water-cooled, twin-cam, four-cylinder racer with shaft drive. Although the machine won its first outing, the only records it set thereafter were those for grief and aggravation. It was the Italian version of the AJS V-4. Thus, Moto Guzzi's next step was a machine that was both more conventional (chain drive) and more exotic (eight cylinders).

Two other Italian factories, Gilera and MV Agusta, the dominant forces in European road racing in the 1950's, had battled each other with air-cooled, double-overhead-camshaft, transverse, four-cylinder racers which were technically first cousins to one other. Moto Guzzi decided to skip the four-cylinder stage and proceed directly to a V-8—water-cooled, with double-overhead-camshaft heads atop each cylinder bank. Moto Guzzi had a stake in creating a design which could be—as the singles had been—developed and refined over a long period of time. More than anything else, Guzzi believed that a shortage of horsepower finally outdated racing machines, so a V-8 design was its insurance against coming up short in the power department. The eight-cylinder design possessed the same advantage over the fours as the fours held over singles and twins: Generally, more cylinders meant higher crankshaft speeds thanks to smaller reciprocating parts, and higher rpm ceilings allowed a multicylinder engine to inhale and explode more fuel and air, thus producing more power than designs of the same displacement with fewer cylinders could deliver.

The numbers were all in favor of the V-8, and the bike caused a sensation when Moto Guzzi unveiled it. But, at the end of 1957 season, before the V-8 could be developed into a winner, all the big names in European Grand Prix racing, save MV Agusta, pulled out. Racing would have to get along without the factories, because sagging motorcycle sales could not bankroll sophisticated creations like the V-8.

The Japanese made the European orthodoxy their own in the 1960's. The situation they faced was not unlike the one confronting the Germans thirty years earlier. The leaders of industry production went unrecognized. This revealed the insularity of the motorcycle world. Europeans and Americans still had difficulty in thinking about Japan as an industrialized nation. Since no one ever saw Japanese motorcycles in Western countries, Occidentals never thought about anyone building motorcycles outside the Western world. And the idea that the Japanese were the world leaders in production at first seemed shocking. To the European and American, the first word which came to mind after the phrase "made in Japan" was "copy." In 1959, when Honda appeared at the Isle of Man with its first road-racing team bikes, Europeans lifted their eyebrows, pointed their fingers, and adopted a polite though patronizing attitude. With shrugs and quick smiles which hinted at contempt, everyone said the Hondas looked like the earlier NSU road racers. Honda just wasn't taken seriously. By 1961 that had changed.

One might believe that Honda came to race in Europe to advertise its name, presence, and motorcycles in the European marketplace. That was plausible enough,

but the commercial line of Honda motorcycles didn't need racing to sell it. Modern-day marketing and development of standard models would suffice. Still, without racing in Europe, there was a good chance that the Japanese could not have broken through that insular smugness, that old-world, old-school business that refused recognition unless one had a closetful of Grand Prix victories and a connection to the grand old names in road racing.

The rapidity with which the Japanese—in the first instance Honda—set about this task stunned most observers. The Europeans had accustomed themselves to that design-and-develop school which was a holdover from the earlier design-it-and-fix-it system. When a new racer came out of a European factory, the last thing one would expect was a winning season. One generally paid loser's dues and went through a period of teething difficulties. When a new machine was created, as in the case of the Guzzi V-8, one might plan, or at least expect, a competitive life of six or eight years. If a manufacturer suffered for a year, as Guzzi did, from crankshaft problems . . . well, such things happened in racing. That wasn't the Japanese way.

At first, European observers couldn't quite adjust. Honda walked new designs in and out as if it were running a Parisian fashion salon. The 1959 125-cc twins went back to Japan from the Isle of Man. Then Honda built a 250 four-cylinder bike which raced once in Japan. It won, and disappeared. Honda came to Europe in 1960 with 125-cc twins completely different from the 1959 machines seen on the Isle of Man. Engines, frames, forks, wheels—nothing was the same. The 1960 four-cylinder 250 racer which Honda took to Europe bore little resemblance to the one raced in Japan in 1959. Honda had a promising season in Europe in 1960. Its machines were reliable and reasonably fast, though they didn't handle very well. At this point, Europeans would have begun long-term development of the machines. Not Honda. It considered the

1960 four-cylinder obsolete and produced a new design.

The new four was based on the 1960 model, but it wasn't merely a refinement. Nine out of ten parts wouldn't swap between the machines. With the new engine went a new frame. Likewise, a new 125 racer was built —in the pattern as its forerunner, but different.

Back to Europe for the 1961 season. Honda won the 125 and 250 World Championships. The Honda team returned to Japan, where for 1962 the factory race department created a 50-cc single for the new 50-cc World Championship series, and built revised 125, 250, and 285 machines. In Europe, Honda won the 1962 125, 250, and 350 World Championships. Honda could afford nearly anything it needed to win—big teams, first-string riders, armies of mechanics. Whatever it took, Honda was willing to do. The accelerated pace never stopped: four-cylinder 125's, the five-cylinder 125's, twin-cylinder 50's, six-cylinder 250's, four-cylinder 350's, six-cylinder 297's, four-cylinder 500's. The Japanese never walked; they ran.

Honda had little choice. It was forced into this seemingly frenzied creation—for which, in all events, it was prepared. The Europeans didn't apply such pressure, to be sure; that fell to Honda's Japanese rivals, Suzuki and Yamaha. The big three continued to build fires under one another. Yamaha and Suzuki marched out new bikes in their own floor shows. Like the Germans, the Japanese aimed at overwhelming by horsepower, and in a three-cornered struggle the Grand Prix bikes got faster and faster. Frame technology and roadholding dragged behind. Only slowly—and sometimes not at all—did the Japanese racing bikes find acceptable road manners.

The Japanese firms ran several races against one another. There was a race from the drawing board to a motorcycle; a race to de-bug quickly; a race to fly the new machine to Europe and get it operational there; and finally *the* race that everyone read about. Honda, wedded to four-stroke engines, struggled against the two-stroke Suzukis and Yamahas, in the 50, 125, and 250 classes, and against MV Agusta in the 350 and 500 classes. Suzuki and Yamaha took the unsupercharged two-stroke engine design out of the major-contender category—to which the East German MZ company had elevated it—and covered the design with World Championships.

Suzuki and Yamaha made such strides with two-stroke technology and with the construction of multicylinder two-strokes, that Honda, in order to keep its four-strokes in the hunt, resorted to engines with more cylinders and higher—positively giddy—redlines. The 1965/66 five-cylinder 125 Honda road racer would rev to 22,000 rpm in an ear-shattering howl, and its top speed broke the 125 mph barrier. The bike was reputed to be so sensitive to the weather that riders joked about the engine going off-song when a cloud intercepted the sun on a bright summer afternoon.

By the time Yamaha and Honda retired their big factory teams in 1967 and 1968, the Grand Prix road-racing world would never be quite the same. The Japanese had created their own racing heritage, complete with books of engineering credits, lists of victories, and hundreds of anecdotes. The Japanese demonstrated that as the world leaders in motorcycle production, they could win almost whenever and whatever they wished. The intensity and thoroughness with which they went at their business dazed Europeans. If an engine wasn't right—or even completely satisfactory—the Japanese built a new, better one in less time and with less fuss than other factories needed for making a minor refinement.

After the Japanese left Europe, when one mentioned them and their Grand Prix racing bikes, the replies still came with a smile. But unlike those benign smiles of 1959, the knowing smiles of 1969 gave evidence that the Japanese had made their point.

G.

american mainstream

American racing grew up on horse tracks—on hot and dusty ovals, marked with holes and ripples, that spread out in front of grandstands and greens all across the United States. The track distances ran from a half-mile to a mile, but the distances were likely to be more precise in the eyes and minds of track promoters than in the harder reality of measuring tapes. Horse tracks speckled the landscape, from big cities to small towns, because horseracing was a bona fide, crowd-gathering sport. Horses, especially if they grew up in rural America, weren't too choosy about the surfaces on which they ran. For that matter, presumably, neither were their owners or riders. It was straightforward local racing, done with few frills and great passion. That's how America went horseracing, and, as it turned out, how Yankees went motorcycle racing as well.

Motorcycles had to adapt to the horsey way of doing things. What a jockey and his horse might consider reasonable riding conditions didn't always strike the motorcycle racer as sound or safe. In the first place, even before 1920, the largest and fastest American racing motorcycles—61-cu. in. V-twin factory specials—could lap a good mile track at about 75 mph, a pace far faster than a horse's. Motorcycles negotiated the wide, flat turns with the machine heeled over, broadsliding in a controlled power drift. The broadsliding technique, which allowed riders to knock off speed and round the corner, was the way to make time if properly done. Good riders could shave off the right amount of momentum through the turn, get traction at exactly the right place coming out of the corner, dial the power back on, and blast down the straight full tilt. No brakes were necessary. Engine-compression braking, coupled with broadsliding, worked better. The trick was to bring traction, speed, and power all into harmony on the proper racing line. With hard, narrow tires, and next-to-nothing suspension, the early dirt-track motorcycles twitched and chattered on choppy surfaces, even when all

elements were in harmony. Hitting a hole while broadsliding might start a plunge into the dust. A hole in the straight could cause the motorcycle to pitch violently, beginning a speed wobble that might sling bike and rider through the outside fence. Horses might live with a rough track; motorcyle racers had to learn to do so.

High speeds and constant sliding raised huge dust storms on the track, and riders were engulfed in churning, eye-searing clouds. They could see their competitors, the turns, even the track surface itself only dimly. Except for the leader, who was clear of the storm until he caught the backmarkers in the field, all racers hurtled along, choking and half-blinded, looking for open space.

It would have mattered little if motorcycling could have found an enthusiastic local government on some friendly island within the United States where a grand European-style event could have been held. Relatively few spectators would have bothered going. Thanks to the Model T, motorcycling in America did not have the numbers to fill grandstands, which left race promoters attempting to flesh out the bleachers with a general audience. They figured that "outsiders" represented as much as eighty percent of their gates. Since motorcycle enthusiasts couldn't support their sport alone, motorcycle racing went where the crowds were: to horse tracks.

Speed mixed with dust on those old mile and half-mile tracks to make a blood sport out of horse-track racing. Fred Ludlow, a member of the Harley-Davidson racing team in the early 1920's, remembered the dust and its dangers: "In the heavy dust of some of the old tracks all we had to follow was the blue exhaust of the fellow ahead. More than once I can remember drifting out until an elbow touched the fence and then pulling back toward the pole. During one race a fellow went through the fence and was killed. We never missed him until after the race, when we were packing up our equipment and happened

99

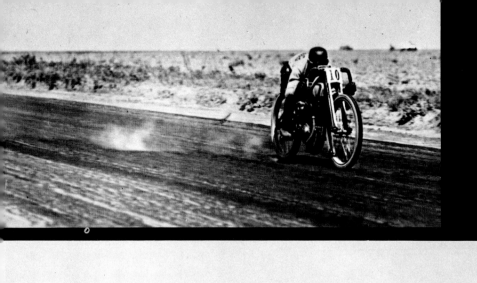

Below: The Dodge City Race, premier American motorcycle event of the nineteen-teens, begins in dust and noise in 1915. Far left: Otto Walker, clinched to his Milwaukee racer for nearly four hours, won the 1915 race. Near left: William Harley flashes a smile at Dodge City in 1920. Winner Jim Davis was Harley-Davidson mounted that year.

Dodge City Daily Globe

DAVIS ON HARLEY TOOK FIRST HONORS IN BIG RACE

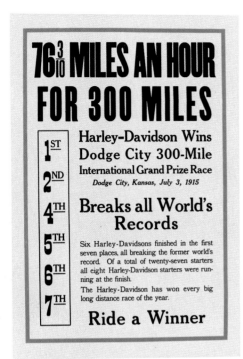

Left: Long-distance racing demonstrated both speed and reliability. Brand competition was intense, so winning riders were not always mentioned. Right: Ralph Hepburn, an early ace, was a factory rider for both Indian and Harley-Davidson.

to count noses, we found him and his machine over on the far side of the track, outside the fence. The spectators had long since gone."

The giant names of American motorcycling—Indian, Harley-Davidson, Excelsior—backed dirt-track racing because they aimed to advertise in front of the largest possible audiences. With factory support came a certain splendor. The best and biggest dirt-track events were organized on a grand scale. The race at Dodge City, Kansas, was run on a huge dirt track, two miles around, for the staggering distance of 300 miles. Winning a machine-thrashing event like Dodge City was unthinkable without direct factory intervention, and even with the manufacturer's support, mere money couldn't buy the 300-mile win. Good teamwork gave a factory a headstart, and Harley-Davidson had the finest racing team in America after World War I. The four or five men on it had to be prepared to ride all kinds of events, but the 300-mile haul at Dodge City presented the longest challenge.

Racing the horse tracks involved places like Greeley, Colorado; Mansfield, Ohio; San Angelo, Texas; Singac, New Jersey; Grand Island, Nebraska; and Huntington, West Virginia. The race distances varied: one, three, five, ten, fifteen, twenty, twenty-five, or fifty miles. On half-mile tracks, the so-called "thirty-fifty singles" ruled after the 61-cu. in. twins proved far too quick and powerful for the smaller ovals. Single-cylinder motorcycles displaced 30.50 cubic inches, hence the name, and they liter-

ally began as 61-cu. in. V-twins with one cylinder lopped off. Later, as the thirty-fifty racing size gained in popularity, brand-new racing singles came off the drawing boards in Milwaukee and Springfield. In order to boost output, Harley-Davidson and Indian produced engines with four valves per cylinder, and the fastest racing machines in America were four-valve singles and eight-valve twins. On mile or longer tracks, professional riders could unholster the 61-cu. in. racing V-twins. Such machines, especially the eight-valve variety, were intended for professional racers only. Sunday amateurs had no business being on the weapons. Rules of competition barred the factory specials from "Stock Machine Contests," which in theory operated as the preserve of amateur racers who were out for a good time in endurance runs, reliability trials, or hill climbs.

Horse-track racing was nibbled down—inch by inch. The racing machines shrank in size. The 30.50 singles were later joined by smaller and slower 21.35-cu. in. hummers. The proliferation of sizes obscured the majestic one-litre V-twins. And Harley-Davidson and Indian tapered off their support of professional riders, though motorcycling still had its brilliant track stars: Johnny Seymour, Jim Davis, Ralph Hepburn, Eddie Brinck, Curly Fredericks, Joe Petrali. These pros raced during motorcycling's economic recession of the 1920's, and then during the Great Depression of the 1930's. Joe Petrali, Harley-Davidson's ace of the 1930's, could do it all—dirt-track racing, board-track racing, and hill climbing—but the times doomed him to be the forgotten man of American motorcycle racing.

Those big, bellowing V-twins remained the fastest two-wheeled racers in America. The hitch was finding a place to unleash their awesome power. Board-track automobile speedways appeared to be the proper setting. These ovals were crossbred creatures varying in length from one mile to two and a half miles. The board surfaces were constructed like the earlier, defunct motordromes, but the big auto speedways were considerably larger (and vastly safer) than the one-third-mile motorcycle saucers. Though the banking didn't generally tilt as steeply as in the old dromes, the racing speeds were terrific anyway. The board speedway at Altoona, Pennsylvania, was a mile and a quarter around, and the promoters chattered, optimistically, about 125-mph laps with motorcycles.

Joe Petrali burst upon the national scene in 1925 by winning the Hundred-Mile National Championship at Altoona. The tough little dark horse from Los Angeles averaged a surprising 100.32 mph. Earlier in the day, Jim Davis, the Harley-Davidson team rider, copped the five-mile at a blistering 110.7 mph. (To put these times in perspective, Peter DePaolo won the 1925 Indianapolis 500 race for automobiles at 101.13 mph.) Skimming over the pine boards at a 100-mph pace, riders were finally free from blinding dust. At the same time, the speedways would not brook inattentive riders. The racers had to stay alert for "heat" in their engines, or any other malfunction, since a failure might be capped with a 125-mph get-off into the splintery woodwork. Riders stayed flat on the tank, tucked in out of the airstream. Largely, this was dictated by centrifugal force, which mashed heads flat against the gas tanks. Some riders put collars around the bottom of the handgrips on their turned-down handlebars to keep the downforce from driving their hands off the grips.

The tracks needed big crowds and gate receipts —a lot of revenue—to survive. As speedways aged, maintenance costs rose. Entire sections had to be replaced. Unlike bricks or asphalt or concrete, wood rotted, and racers couldn't set new speed records on shaky, splintery surfaces. As urban populations grew, speedways found themselves surrounded by neighbors who could live without the excitement of racing. When the Great Depression came, the board tracks folded.

Hill climbing, by contrast, grew as an attraction

during the 1920's and 1930's. It seemed a natural for American motorcycle enthusiasts. The basic requirement was a big, steep hill, accessible by road for the convenience of spectators. No one had to build a racecourse, because the object was the straight-up charge on natural terrain. String and flags defined the corridor to the top, and within these boundaries the motorcycles eventually established a path of sorts. The machines were supposed to race the clock one by one to the summit, though most contestants earned their placings on the distance they climbed before they were stopped by the incline and the pitted terrain.

Hill climbing was spectacular, easy to understand, and never dull. Local motorcycle clubs, organized around a hometown dealer, had all the resources necessary to stage a climb. Most events were small, friendly gatherings of local townspeople who arrived in Model T Fords with their families and picnic baskets to watch the fun.

Although there were hill-climb racers who rode professionally (Joe Petrali for Excelsior and then Harley-Davidson, Orie Steele for Indian) and—later—readymade hill-climbing bikes, the great body of hill artists was made up of private owners who began with near-standard models and bit by bit built their way toward specialized hill climbers. The amateur could race what he owned, since there were classes for almost all sizes of production-based motorcycles. Compared to any other kind of real competition, hill climbing was an inexpensive, low-pressure sport.

While hill climbing had much vitality, dirt-track racing remained sluggish, a reflection of the continuing withdrawal of factory support, the tightening economic

Left: Hill climbing was largely an amateur preserve of motorcycle sport in the 1920's. Easy to organize and understand, hill climbing attracted local townspeople as spectators. They would muster out on Sunday afternoons with picnic baskets and watch the motorcycles attack a well-known hill. Right: Board-track races were far more difficult to stage. These professional events took place inside great board-track palaces. With no danger from dust, the racers could squirt their motorcycles to three-figure race averages. Close-formation drafting and team riding eased the strain on engines.

conditions, and the lack of any new talent. Only a few racing stars could win enough to make a living after they were squeezed off the full-time factory payrolls.

By the late twenties, the manufacturers and the American Motorcycle Association, the new race-sanctioning organization in the United States, decided that racing had to be de-professionalized and de-specialized. It was decreed that the factory-racing machines—those expensive specials for professional riders—had to be abandoned. Without substantial factory bankrolling, fully professionalized racing could not be sustained, and the American factories weren't interested in paying anymore. If the manufacturers and professionals couldn't afford to race, then the rules had to be changed so that amateurs could—whereby the sport would be saved. The AMA established Class C racing (A and B were the old categories for special factory-racing machines). Class C was supposed to be grass-roots racing, using road-going machines. They had to be stock designs— as manufactured, catalogued, and sold.

Of all standard machines in the United States in the 1930's the most natural motorcycles to race were the 45-cu. in. V-twins—Harley-Davidson's W model and Indian's Scout. These motorcycles were light, compared to the larger American monsters, but sufficiently powerful to make racing them interesting. With Milwaukee and Springfield turning them out, they were plentiful and inexpensive, especially when picked up second-hand. Enthusiasts could try racing without buying anything more special than his own road bike. During the week, he could ride his machine on the street. On a Sunday, he could go to the races, strip his motorcycle down at the track—yanking off the headlight and pulling the hinge-pin out of the rear fender— and race. This amateur-style racing, coupled with a break in America's long Depression fever, ended the somnambulism. And racing on horse tracks was back.

Before long, Indian and Harley-Davidson slipped in the back door of Class C racing by building racing models based on their 45-cu. in. street machines. Harley-Davidson introduced its WR racer in 1941. The sidevalve V-twin had a warmed-up engine, with racing camshafts, a higher compression ratio, and a crankshaft that ran on ball bearings instead of roller bearings. One could overdignify the WR by calling it an all-out factory racer. The thing wore footboards and had a hand shift for its wide-ratio gearbox. The suspension operated at one end only. Simple coil springs allowed some movement in the front forks, but the rear wheel and axle were bolted directly into the frame. Not a factory special like Harley-Davidson's old professional bikes, the WR was just a stripped street bike modified for racing; the factory saved the owner the bother of racifying his road machine.

On dirt tracks, over ripples, holes, and bumps, those little racing Indians and Harley-Davidsons would jump, buck, and slide sideways. But since no one had ever ridden anything that handled much better, riders accepted the lurching as normal. The earlier Class A motorcycles— more powerful, lighter, and smaller—may have handled better, but the 45's weren't ridden the same way the rapier-like 30.50's had been. The Class C racing 45's just couldn't be managed with those narrow, dropped bars, which early dirt-track racers seemed to inherit from racing bicycles. Most riders preferred wider, more upright bars, so that the 45's could be levered and muscled through corners. Gone, too, were the adder-gauge tires on which genuine factory racing bikes rolled. On the 45's, riders mounted wide-sectioned tires—4.00 or 4.50 in 18- and 19-inch sizes—in order to aid handling. With low pressures, the tires would flex enough to give a crude kind of added suspension. Such was the state of the art in 1941—and in 1947, when motorcycle racing resumed after the wartime blackout.

The 200-Mile National Championship race had been transferred to Daytona Beach from Savannah, Geor-

107

Manx Nortons invaded the old
Daytona Beach course in the postwar era.
Top: Dick Klamfoth (2) tucked in
at the oceanside start. Above: Klamfoth,
winner in 1951, posed with runners-up
Billy Mathews (98) and Bill Tuman (51).
Right: Dirt tracking. The Manx
in a rigid frame dashes to the flag.

gia, in 1937. The old Daytona Beach course, as lengthened and altered in 1948, was a sand-and-macadam hybrid. It was neither a road course nor a dirt track. The backstretch reeled out for two miles on a narrow, bumpy, and relatively straight piece of macadam which ended in the south turn—or, more properly, the south turns. One steeply banked turn dropped downhill and led into another, mildly banked corner that routed traffic onto the oceanfront beach straightaway. The charge up the beach ended at the banked north turn, which, on a 500-foot radius, climbed uphill and hooked into the backstretch. The beach course was something of a board speedway without boards, done in patches of asphalt and sand. And coquina rock. Workmen cut turns out of the sand dunes and topped the assembled turns with crushed coquina laid over clay. The makeshift clay-and-crushed rock surfacing, reputed to be fairly resistant to breaking up, could not be applied to some parts of the turns because the tides would have washed it away.

The water, as well as the rutted sand, presented a few problems of its own. Salt spray fogged up goggles and had to be knuckled off at the right time. If an anxious rider, buzzing up the beach, tried to wipe his goggles too soon, he would only blur his vision more by smearing the still wet spray. One had to wait until the salt had caked, then rub slits in the film.

Ed Kretz, the winner of the 1937 inaugural, sped home at a 74.10-mph average, though in truth he could have gone faster had the tide not slowed him. Thanks to a misreading of tide tables, the end of the race dovetailed nicely with the incoming tide, and Kretz finished the race almost motorboating. By 1948, on a revised course, the winning speed was up almost 10 mph, Floyd Emde collecting victory at an 84.01-mph clip. The American 45's, both Indian and Harley-Davidson, got faster and better. The V-twins controlled Daytona until 1949, when a British interloper from European Grand Prix circuits arrived.

Dick Klamfoth, a wiry, blond, eighteen-year-old farm boy from Groveport, Ohio, and a classic British single-cylinder road-racing bike made an unlikely duo to stagger the American V-twins on their oceanfront course. Norton motorcycles landed in the postwar United States as a partial consequence of the British economic-recovery program which sent massive exports abroad. The AMA approved for competition the single-overhead-camshaft 500 Norton International, which the British factory supplied in two versions, one with a lighting set and road equipment, the other a stripped-down racing model. Billy Mathews, Canada's leading racer, demonstrated the potency of the Norton International by winning the 1941 Daytona event, yet the Yankees remained skeptical. Floyd Emde

Right:
Harley-Davidson rider
Mark Brelsford
at speed. A motorcycle
racer depends on his
timing, balance, hand-to-eye
co-ordination, and
mental coolness during
close-quarter maneuvering.

ward movement of using the hand-shift levers. Not only could Klamfoth and the other Norton riders shift more rapidly, they could keep both hands on the bars for better control through the sand traps, where, without a good line and plenty of speed, an engine could bog. Klamfoth, both hands on the bars and shifting quickly, rode precisely.

The rough macadam backstretch pounded the Norton's plunger frame, breaking half the tubing that carried the rear plungers; the Norton's heralded handling disappeared with the fractures. Nevertheless, Manx Nortons became the motorcycles to beat at Daytona. Klamfoth won in 1949 at a record 86.42 mph, nosing out fellow Norton rider Billy Mathews by 14 seconds. In 1950, Mathews won and Klamfoth was second, and the average speed climbed to 88.44 mph. Klamfoth added a second victory in 1951, when his Manx dashed to the checkered flag 20 seconds ahead of Bobby Hill, who was aboard another Norton single. Klamfoth scored a third win in 1952, with the British double-knocker turning back the opposition again.

Young Klamfoth was a "professional" motorcycle racer. Motorcycle racing was his consuming avocation, it ate up his weekends and late evenings. For Daytona Speed Week in March, Klamfoth would drive off to Florida and meet Beart and the American distributors for Norton, the Indian Sales Corporation. Pulling in early, he would help Beart and Jimmy Hill, chief engineer for the Indian company, prepare the Nortons. At first, there was little for the Ohio teen-ager to do. Beart was cordial enough, but he wasn't about to let some young farm boy from America's

middleland go playing about inside a Manx Norton engine. Beart would, however, entrust Klamfoth with the attachment of number plates and suchlike. The Ohioan, who had a knack for things mechanical, observed much and learned quickly—from both Beart and Hill.

Klamfoth schooled well. He had to, if he wanted to keep his Manx engine running crisply for the rest of the season. He was given his Daytona machines, and for the balance of the year the Ohio rider was his own engineer and mechanic. That meant rebuilding Nortons during the weekday evening hours on the farm, dashing off to some Sunday flat-track race, racing, and then highballing it back to the farm. No motel or swank surroundings, and no luxuries. Winners might make $50 or $100 on a Sunday flat-track event. National-championship events paid more, but the smaller flat-track races kept the new professionals going. In his best professional season, Klamfoth grossed $9,500 in forty-odd races.

The plunger-frame Norton took poorly to American flat tracking. Road-racing purists would have been horrified to know that a Manx Norton, raised on the hallowed roads of the Isle of Man, would be asked to broadslide its way around a dusty, dirty, American half-mile track. But Klamfoth adapted the Manx to American conditions, building the twin-cam engine into the rigid frame of an earlier Norton roadster. This creative adaptation stepped gingerly over and around, or on, the "stock-components" rule, but no one really objected, since the Norton was never quite the threat on mile and half-mile

dirt tracks that it was at Daytona. Its narrow power band and lack of low-speed torque made the British intruder an underdog on soft dirt tracks.

The lessons of Daytona weren't lost on Harley-Davidson, which came to the beach in 1953 with a new "KR" racer: swinging-arm frame, telescopic forks with internal coil springs and hydraulic damping, and a new 45-cu. in., sidevalve, V-twin unit with foot-shift transmission. Midnight oil blazed when the Harley-Davidson faithful discovered that their new KR racers neither handled as well nor had as much power as the old WR models. The macadam section of the course, grown rougher, caused some heart-stopping wobbles at 100-mph speeds.

Experimentation began on the spot. Frames were cut and changed to increase the front-fork rake so as to stabilize high-speed handling. After a few hectic days of frame snipping and welding, the handling smoothed out. Paul Goldsmith won the race for Harley-Davidson with tricks out of the Norton bag. His 37-hp KR model actually had three or four fewer horsepower than a good WR racer. However, the new foot-shift, close-ratio, four-speed gearbox allowed the KR to out-accelerate the earlier V-twin easily. The KR won on the Norton formula: better suspension and running gear, and superior power transmission with no more—perhaps less—horsepower.

Harley-Davidson's real interest in frame technology dated from its efforts to improve handling of the early KR models. Before that time, Americans considered the frame and forks as merely the most convenient way to hold the engine and wheels together. The early KR frames were convertibles. If a man was going dirt tracking, which called for a solid rear end, he simply unbolted the rear subframe that carried the swinging-arm rear suspension and attached in its place the rigid-frame section. From that single starting point, Harley-Davidson pursued frame development down different paths, as the increasingly specialized demands of different kinds of racing (road racing and dirt tracking) led to quite dissimilar frames.

In the 1950's, riders began to become more sharply aware of differences that might result from subtle changes in the "simple" rigid-frame flat-track motorcycles. They showed more concern with frame geometry, rake and trail, center of gravity, wheelbase, engine position, weight transfer, and fork lengths. Little adjustments counted—in the rider's mind and on the track. He might fit longer or shorter forks, drop the rear end or pick it up a bit, shorten the wheelbase or lengthen it, and on and on. No one had seriously considered laying the rigid-frame tracker aside and trying to make a swinging-arm frame work on the dirt ovals. No one, at least, had found a workable solution. In bald-headed theory, a frame that suspended the rear wheel as well as the front had the potential to increase traction at the rear tire. In practice it didn't work. Those who thought about such a change speculated that a dirt-track swinging-arm frame would operate with a different set of engineering rules. Those who knew the prescriptions for a good rigid-frame dirt-tracker weren't interested in experimenting; time could better be spent dealing with more obvious problems. And so flat-track racers stayed on their hard-tailed frames until the mid-1960's, when a bright, experienced dirt-track artist, Dick Mann, started the swinging-arm revolution.

The more the racers of the 1950's fiddled and modified their motorcycles, the larger the spots they wore into the Class C rules. The official rulebook still endorsed grass-roots racing and frowned upon alterations of stock components, save in the interest of safety. But racing had its own inexorable logic—to go faster— and this goal frayed the rulebooks and bent the sentences therein.

A dirt-track racer had to know his tires, and in the 1950's racers used certain tires on particular kinds of dirt surfaces. Traction and control were the objects of the ongoing experiment. Tire changes were about the last big variable a rider could control at trackside. The tread patterns, the rubber's softness or hardness, the condition of tread edges, the shape of the tires, the amount of and kind of wear—all counted. The rider had to be able to read the racetrack surface, and to know how hard and tacky or soft and cushy the surface in the groove (the racing line) was, or might become if weather or racing conditions altered the surface or the groove itself. The racing didn't demand unerring precision in the selection of tires, but no rider could make a gross error and still win. A track-wise professional might not slip the rear wheel, carrying his tire choice, into his motorcycle until the last possible second before the start of an important dirt-track event. Sometimes professionals held a staring stand-off in the pits, a battle of wits and nerve that went on until the final call to the line-up forced action. One year, late in the 1950's, at the Five-Mile National Championship in Minneapolis, two Harley-Davidson veterans, Joe Leonard and Carroll Resweber, sat around eying one another in this way, each with his rear wheel missing, each believing that he knew the winning tire combination, each trying to batter the other psy-

chologically, and each determined not to give his secret away. That day Resweber won, but the win wasn't all hidden in the tire selection. Resweber, approaching his peak, was simply and directly almost unbeatable.

Carroll Resweber was not just another champion. He had a special gift for motorcycle racing. The telegraphy between Resweber and a racing motorcycle operated in a dimension apart from normal human experience. He could do things with a motorcycle that passed beyond the understanding of many of his contemporaries. A motorcycle could heave, jump, chatter, and try to swap ends on a mile or half-mile track; but if the motorcycle would go faster round a track in a series of wags and hiccups, Resweber could, and would, ride the thing that way, and fool everyone with his tidy style. Resweber's body worked with the greatest economy of movement, with an uncanny, slow-motion pace, though the motorcycle under him might dance to a St. Vitus's jig around the track.

Motorcycle racing never stepped out of Resweber's mind. He thought constantly of how a machine and rider might go more quickly around a dirt track. An experimentalist, he might consider several ways of setting a machine up for a track. He could try alternatives that didn't occur to others because he could ride those alternative set-ups and others couldn't. Resweber could rocket out of corners because under acceleration his motorcycles transferred so much weight back through the rear tire that his equipment got tremendous traction and "bite." It left the front end of the motorcycle very light, and Resweber mastered the art of turning and controlling a feather-light front end. No one else could get away with it.

The gasping spectacle of dirt-track racing belied the scientific approach which Carroll Resweber and others brought to it. The major dirt-track events plugged into the state-fair circuits in the Midwest. Motorcycle racing was still going where the crowds were. The spectators came for the thrills-chills-and-spills matinee show; they couldn't see the minds behind this racing. To them, mile or half-mile racing was all derring-do. But the science was there—subtle, intricate, hidden in the machines.

Racers like Carroll Resweber were likewise intricate. Resweber was hardly a wordy man; he was, in fact, downright taciturn. He appeared to have a hard and brittle brand of competitiveness. If he couldn't be the best at a certain task or calling, he didn't want to do it. Resweber seemed a self-contained, tightly knit person who kept his own counsel and who, beyond a certain level, was not knowable, even to those who raced against him. Everyone, however, could recognize Resweber's enormous desire to win. On that matter he needn't utter a word.

Resweber's silence served him well. He never revealed a dangling psychological end, or showed a loose thread which a competitor might pick up and start pulling. Sphinx-like, he watched and listened to his adversaries, looking for flaws in their riding and cracks in their psyches. Resweber turned the collected information over in his mind, examining it, until at last he decided how to exploit the flaws and widen the cracks. At least that's how some of his rivals believed he maneuvered and worked them, time and again. If he ever doubted his own commanding mastery, Resweber lock-boxed those doubts from view. Behind his guarded exterior lurked a psychological-warfare expert who knew that his power came both from what he could do and what others thought he could do.

Resweber grew to racing maturity on mile and half-mile tracks, and the ease and grace with which he rode made him the AMA National Champion for an unprecedented four straight years: 1958, 1959, 1960, and 1961. And his talent continued to grow. He began to adapt to pavement racing, which at first had confounded him. When he recalibrated his timing for road racing, his dirt-track smoothness, economy, and speed suddenly appeared on road courses. That transition amazed those who thought that Europeans owned road racing as surely as Americans owned dirt-track racing and that never the two should meet, the talents necessary to each somehow being separate. For those who cared to notice, Resweber scuttled the notion. His studied approach to racing, his capacity to experiment, his innate talent and ferocious passion to excel —created a racing brilliance, singular and dazzling.

Carroll Resweber was America's last uncut champion. He didn't just win; he dominated. He was a whole champion in a way others later couldn't be. American racing began to diversify in the 1960's, and by the end of the decade, specialists had sectioned off the American racing scene. No one man could dominate all of racing the way Resweber had. Specialists abounded, and the chase for the National Championship became a contest between the best of the good all-rounders among the specialists.

The Resweber era ended at the close of the 1962 season at a dusty half-mile track at Lincoln, Illinois. He was there to sew up his fifth straight national title. Out in practice, as Dick Klamfoth recalled, he and Resweber circulated together on the track. Ruts laced the surface, the dust billowed up from the track and hung in the air. Resweber and Klamfoth had a half-lap between themselves and a group of other riders. No flagmen warned the pair of the danger ahead in the swirling dust. Other riders and machines were down, sprawled on the track. Klamfoth, trailing Resweber, remembers seeing the Harley-Davidson rider suddenly dart left, and a split-second later Klamfoth saw what Resweber had seen: a motorcycle down on the track in the dust. The tangled pile-up inside that duster snuffed out one life, knocked Klamfoth out cold for hours, and sent Carroll Resweber, badly injured, into retirement. The American mainstream disappeared in the Illinois dust.

American racing never found another Carroll Resweber, who was both the champion and the best.

7.

It was the simple, undecorated truth. Motorcycle development was stunted. Mechanically, motorcycles were progressing by inches, checked by the lack of money in manufacturers' bank accounts, by the conservative impulses of the makers, and by economic conditions which strangled boldness.

Of course, motorcycles were better than before, but in no way had they progressed as automobiles had. In America in 1939, trying to sell an automobile without an electric starter would have been absurd, but motorcyclists accepted the fact that one kicked a motorcycle into life. Spring-frame progress stopped in the United States in the early 1920's, when Indian discontinued this option. Aggravated by increasing weight and power, the costly feature worked imperfectly, and it would have cost a lot more to make it work well. What customers might not buy, Indian was not going to develop.

Motorcyclists accepted the little fragilities of motoring life. Owners of four-cylinder Indians, for example, understood that crankshaft assemblies would not tolerate rider abuse. Engines had a degree of durability that would have clanged the death knell for an auto maker. Technically, the most advanced motorcycles weren't being built in the United States. British and continental makers were fabricating motorcycles, which, on paper at least, were nice pieces of hardware. But exotic models put together in tiny lots hardly influenced the general run, which had rigid frames, girder forks, chain drive, miserable electrics, mildly tuned sidevalve or overhead-valve four-stroke engines, or sluggish two-stroke units, with capacities ranging from 100 cc to 500 cc.

Ralph Rogers, the Indian company's postwar president, was either a wide-eyed visionary, or a sucker for an English accent. The idea of a "gentleman's motorcycle" possessed this Yankee, who looked to England and the British vertical twins for inspiration. Compared to the Triumph Speed Twin, for example, American motorcycles seemed clubby, crude, and obese. The American V-twins —to say nothing of the Indian four-cylinder—had become oversized and overweight. The future of motorcycling, the argument ran, lay in attracting people a social cut above the plain, blue-collared fellows who had supported motorcycling through the lean years.

To draw a new clientele, the sport needed a new sort of motorcycle. Light, responsive, smooth, stylish, refined—those were the characteristics a gentleman's motorcycle should have. Perhaps Rogers should have really been in the sports-car import business, since his vision applied more to four-wheeled performance vehicles than to two-wheelers. Rogers got his British-style motorcycle, and it was a disaster. The 74-cu. in. V-twin joined the pre-war Indian four-cylinder and the old 45-cu. in. V-twin on the discontinued list. The new British-pattern bike, with an overhead-valve, vertical-twin engine, four-speed, foot-shift gearbox, telescopic front forks, and plunger frame was rushed into production late in 1948.

The new Indian Scout, later enlarged to the 30.50-cu. in. Warrior, looked great and ran well, but not for long. Transmissions failed, crankshafts failed, ignition systems failed. By 1950 the machines had created so many service and warranty problems that the Indian company lay mortally wounded. The twin spiked the firm in 1949, though it was not until 1953 that the last American Indian dribbled off the line.

Had the Scout-Warrior been as good a motorcycle as the Triumph Speed Twin, Indian might have prospered. The Triumph vertical twin had changed the whole direction of motorcycle design. Certainly there had been engines of similar layout earlier: Peugeot of France built a successful racer in the 1920's, and Triumph constructed an experimental vertical twin in 1913, but the first vertical twin to catch the imagination of the motor-

Opening pages: The 650-cc Triumph Thunderbird of 1950 preserved the archetypical form of the original prewar Speed Twin. The spring hub provided rear suspension and a few handling peculiarities as well. Perfectly proportioned Thunderbird became the best-known "foreign" motorcycle in postwar America.

cycling public was the 500-cc Speed Twin introduced in England late in 1937.

Triumph's twin, however, had its origin in a four-cylinder engine, built by the Ariel factory in Birmingham, England. Ariel was run by Jack Sangster, and he brought Edward Turner out of the obscurity of a small South London motorcycle shop to work in the Ariel drawing office alongside Valentine Page and Bert Hopwood. Those names—Turner, Page, Hopwood—all proved important in the development and elaboration of the British vertical twin. But at the time, they were more concerned at Ariel with designing a four-cylinder for Jack Sangster.

The square-four arrangement as proposed by Turner was a compact 500-cc design with chain driven overhead camshaft. Essentially the design comprised two vertical twins with their crankshafts set across the frame and connected by gears, with all four cylinders running in a monobloc casting. In the course of time the Ariel four increased in size to 600 cc, and eventually to a one-litre engine. In the process it lost its overhead camshaft and gained pushrods and rockers. Though the Square Four lived on in revised form into the 1950's, Ariel didn't produce it in any quantity.

Around the middle of 1930, just before the 500 four went into production, Sangster told his experimental shop to extract the front crankshaft and pistons from one of the prototype fours—just to see what would happen. That left the engine as a rudimentary 250-cc vertical twin. In the presence of Page and Hopwood, the converted engine was started. And it ran so smoothly that Sangster shouted in astonishment: "What the hell have we been playing around with fours for?"

That was a good question, and one which Valentine Page carried with him when he left Ariel's employ to join Triumph at Coventry. And there, unsurprisingly, one of his first designs was a 650-cc vertical twin, which was introduced in 1933. It was the first of its type to be offered to the British public. But if Page was ready to design a vertical twin, and Triumph ready to build it, the motorcycling public wasn't prepared to buy it. The motorcycle was a heavy, ponderous thing, hard on the eyes. Had it been an appealing, lithe machine, success still would not have stuck to it. The British consumer, fighting his way back from economic disaster, remained tightfisted with his motoring cash, and old-fashioned singles better fitted the needs and temperament of the times.

By 1935 the Triumph company was doing better with its automobiles than with its bicycles and motorcycles. It decided to focus all efforts on cars and sell off the two-wheeled lines. Jack Sangster bought Triumph and added it to his Ariel holdings, though he kept production of the two makes entirely separate. Sangster then appointed Edward Turner as the designer and manager of the reconstituted Triumph Engineering Company, with instructions to get Triumph back in the forward ranks of the motorcycle market. Turner slicked up the existing range of single-cylinder Triumphs and dropped the Page-designed vertical twin, replacing it with a 500 vertical twin from his own hand.

Brought out in late 1937, it was an immediate success. The public stampeded to place orders. The new twin succeeded brilliantly where the earlier one had languished. The Turner machine came to market in better economic times, and that was an advantage. And the Speed Twin had a purity of line and angle about it. It looked right, exactly right: light and agile, lithe and sleek. The engine comprised two vertical singles running inside a common crankcase, with the pistons rising and falling together, but firing alternately. The long-stroke twin (63 mm x 80 mm) would spin to 6,000 rpm, at which point it developed about 28 hp, and at 360 pounds it was five pounds lighter than the single-cylinder 500 it was replac-

*Above and right: BSA Gold
Star was the most widely revered
British single in the United
States. But no amount of emotion
could save the classic 500
singles; the future belonged to
vertical twins and multis.
The future wasn't "streamlined."
Left: Triumph eventually
lost its full-bodied nacelle. And a
swinging-arm rear suspension
replaced the old spring hub.*

ing in the model line-up. The frame was nothing new. It was rigid and had girder forks which dealt with bumps by means of coil springing and friction dampers.

The Speed Twin spoke "performance," and the Tiger 100, a tuned-up version of the new motorcycle, appeared in the 1939 catalogues. The Tiger 100 would humble other sports 500's, including the Norton International. And the Triumph was, in the context of its day, oil-tight—which is to say it leaked a little. The road performance did not make a mockery of its reliability; British customers weren't left standing at the roadside in a fume. Turner had created a lively, well-mannered motorcycle which was a thing of beauty.

The Speed Twin was only the beginning of the vertical twin. Bert Hopwood, one of the witnesses to the Ariel four-to-twin experiment, had meanwhile transferred to BSA, where he was soon joined by Turner. For BSA, Turner designed another vertical twin which reached production just after World War II as the 500-cc A7. However, this machine was less successful than the Triumph, and the sales of the BSA 500 were overtaken by a 650 BSA vertical twin—the Golden Flash A10—which was the work of Bert Hopwood. Later Hopwood engineered the 500 vertical twin which replaced Turner's first BSA effort. And over at Ariel, Valentine Page busied himself in the drawing room, and the result was a 500 Ariel vertical twin. Later, when Jack Sangster sold both his Ariel and Triumph factories to BSA, a 650 Ariel-cum-BSA twin emerged.

Hopwood left the BSA group in the 1950's and proceeded to the Norton factory, a move that resulted in the Norton Dominator 88. The 500 vertical twin grew as the years passed, and in much-modified form later it powered the 750 and 850 Norton Commandos. So that day in 1930 when Jack Sangster's curiosity led to the Ariel experiment may have been the most important day in British motorcycling.

When Indian's last whoop was nothing more than an echo rattling around inside a silent factory, Rogers might have paused to reflect whether Indian could have endured if the 1949 Scout had been a sound machine. The answer probably was yes. Whether gentlemen would have bought "gentlemen's motorcycles" was less likely. As to whether the whole gentleman's-motorcycle concept was out of place in late-1940's America—the answer to that very clearly was yes.

A different kind of motorcycle, British-style, did not produce a new clientele. There were Harley-Davidson riders, Indian riders, and foreign-bike riders. They all came from the same pool. The Triumph, easily the best-known foreign motorcycle in America, had its partisans. But the fact that they rode Triumphs did not make them gentlemen in the way Ralph Rogers thought. In hard truth, any resurgence in the American motorcycle market, beyond expected levels, had more to do with pent-up consumer demand left over from wartime austerity than from a rediscovery of the motorcycle sport by millions of Americans, or a shift in the social basis of motorcycling. Some members of America's white-collar, professional middle class had bought into motorcycling, but they were very few, and imported machines had no corner on that segment of the market.

Before World War II, when motorcycling had an "image problem," industry spokesmen urged motorcyclists to clean up and quiet down on the road. After the war, spokesmen could worry about roving bands of motorcycle gangs who allegedly kicked down towns while guzzling beer and chasing local womenfolk, or worse. Nothing could be much farther from the concept of gentlemen on motorcycles. The motorcycle establishment responded with much hand-wringing and countless words of explanation and apology, but the "bad image" would not fade. The situation was bewildering. If one owned a mo-

NSU was once a great power in motorcycling. The efforts of the Neckarsulm firm peaked in the mid-1950's, shortly before the German company it went into the four-wheeled business. The 250-cc Super Max featured a pressed-steel frame, swinging arm, and front forks. NSU's 250-cc single-cylinder engine had an overhead camshaft driven by two sets of eccentrics and connecting rods. In the fifties, the well-made, dependable NSU attracted an American clientele that wanted the fun of motorcycling without oil leaks, baffling electrics, and other bothers.

torcycle, others demanded to know why one wasn't actually a social renegade, a low-brow who, in concert with others, raped and pillaged small communities. Had one been an asthma-stricken 97-pound weakling, there might have been something strangely flattering about being taken for a hell-for-leather baddie, but generally the situation was simply confounding. There were isolated events of motorcycle gangs doing real harm, but those events became elaborated, embellished, and scaled up as they passed through the newspapers, weekly news magazines, and finally Hollywood. That insistent progression had more to do with postwar America than motorcycling, though it never struck motorcyclists that their special problem had larger roots elsewhere.

In the years following World War II, Americans wanted things and security. Eager to get on with the business of living, which had been interrupted by global war, returning veterans rushed to college or raced directly off to make a living and enjoy the good life. They wanted lives free from uproars, uncertainties, and discontents; they wanted that quiet, orderly life promised in *The Saturday Evening Post*. Americans were prosperous in a way they never had been before. The war had brought scarcities, and for the first time in a generation postwar Americans had money to buy things. For some, the period of deprivation stretched all the way back to 1930. In the postwar period, many material goods had status marks on them, and others seemed to possess a reassuring permanence. Americans went on a house-building and -buying spree. Consumers pounded after automobiles. Who, outside of confirmed motorcycle enthusiasts, would have wanted a motorcycle? The American car was part of that stable, prosperous world of the 1920's, which people of the late 1940's wished to re-create. A motorcycle suggested sub-achievement in an acquisitive society.

It was also an America with a marshaled mind,

both tense and weary after a war, intolerant of deviations from normal standards. The American public had just fought through a war, carrying a vision of a normalized postwar country; with peace, no one wanted to see much of anything in America out of place. It was no time for free-ranging, inquiring minds; nonconformists operated at their own peril. "Law-abiding" meant just that. In this setting, Americans had a very brittle tolerance for outlaws—motorcycle or otherwise—and they were quite prepared to believe, perhaps expect, the worst from anything the least tainted with law-breaking. Had motorcycles been status-seekers' objects, that might have mollified the finger-pointing at motorcycling. But, in America, Buicks had what motorcycles needed.

European motorcycling developed an image problem of its own in the 1950's—as soon as automobiles became achievable goals for the motoring public. In the fifties and sixties, the transportation side of motorcycling fell away, leaving the hardened sports, whom everyone thought were a bit thick in the head. But at the close of World War II, automobiles seemed a piper's dream, and those interested in motorized private transportation scarcely thought beyond motorcycles.

In England, a good deal of the motoring public was the motorcycle-consuming public. British factories concentrated on utilitarian mounts for postwar customers, but interest in big motorcycles, as the last step before automobiles, remained high. But British consumers still waited in long lines to buy big road machines, which went first to the export trade. The Germans, likewise rebuilding, re-established private transport on two wheels. The NSU company, with new facilities at Neckarsulm, geared up to produce small motorcycles and mopeds. Their under-200-cc machines sold well, and the 1953 NSU Quickly, a tiny two-stroke moped, broke all sales records in Germany. In 1953 NSU also brought out its Max model, powered by a four-stroke engine which was packaged in a pressed-steel frame with leading-link front forks and swinging-arm rear suspension. The NSU single joined the 250-cc BMW single, and the 500-cc and 600-cc BMW opposed twins. The Germans reached zenith in transport-motorcycling very quickly.

If one counted silence, smoothness, quality finishing, and reliability as the marks of a gentlemanly machine, then the Indian company should have patterned its postwar motorcycles on the German examples. The Germans built machines that worked in ways that other motorcycles did not. One could set off on a BMW, or an NSU, or a Zundapp, and know that it would perform as reliably as an automobile of the period. In that sense, the postwar German machines, 175 cc and larger, were among the first nonretarded motorcycles. They did not leak oil; the Germans accurately machined the mating surfaces and used good gaskets and modern oil seals. Engines were built carefully and ran smoothly. Nuts did not vibrate off bolts, a common occurrence with most motorcycles. When one turned on the headlights, light flooded the road at night, with precious few collapses into unexpected darkness. Some postwar machines, especially British, could have unpleasant surprises lurking in the electrical system. Ammeters on British machines failed with perverse reliability, and the Joseph Lucas name was much taken in vain on many a dark and rainy night.

The Germans had been wiped out by the war. Not only had the factories been bombed and shelled, but in some cases the winning parties carried off machine tools and equipment as war damages. This process seemed to work to the Germans' advantage in the end. They got back into motorcycle production with new tools under new roofs and they produced new designs. Yet the German edge went beyond newness. More than anyone else, the Germans took seriously the idea of building modern transportation machines, and this meant that the motorcycle in all its aspects had to continue to function with a minimum amount of fussing on the part of its owners. For example, the Germans invariably protected the final drive on their motorcycles, whether by means of a driveshaft on the BMW's, or fully enclosed chainguards on the Zundapps and NSU's, eliminating or minimizing chain wear and adjustment. And German makers prided themselves on one-kick starting, the last refinement before electric starting. That kind of engineering suggested that German factories really didn't expect their customers to love the machine, or love it well enough to brook much bother. The central function of the machine was efficient transportation. And so German motorcycles were the only machines one could think of as two-wheeled automobiles. There wasn't much passion to them, but reliability and dependability the German motorcycles had.

American riders differed from British and European riders in the way they used their motorcycles on the roads. An American was likely to pick the fastest, straightest way between two points and, with the throttle grip twisted almost to its stop, or against it, proceed with very great haste. In an effort to minimize the shattering of engines, American manufacturers had long taken out insurance in the form of large, slow-turning configurations. British and European machines had substantially smaller engines than the big American touring bikes, and the smaller the engine, the more vulnerable it was to that peculiar American brand of destruction. Small German machines—BMW, NSU, and Zundapp singles ranging from 175 to 250 cc—had the best survival rates in the United States for such pint-sized motorcycles. The German, with autobahns in their past and future, assumed riders would flail engines on fast stretches. Of the countries in Europe, Germany's driving conditions—at their best—most closely approximated those of the American scene. Though the

When small Italian motorcycles landed on American shores in the 1950's, many came with clip-on bars and gas tanks that advertised the makers' connection to European road racing. The 200-cc Ducati Elite wore a positively bizarre fuel tank. Bevel gears and a towershaft ran the single overhead camshaft. Though quick and agile, they had the hardest saddles, harshest suspensions, and strangest electrics in motorcycling.

Moto Parilla prospered in the 1950's and died in the 1960's. An elevated chain-driven camshaft on the left side of the engine operated the valves via short pushrods and rockers. Tuned versions of the 175-cc, 200-cc, and 250-cc singles were very fast. The Parilla Grand Sport (below) was leader of the marque.

250-cc NSU Super Max was a real flyer, speed and power weren't the selling points of German machines. Rather, it was their substance, that kind of density which suggested that a nine-pound hammer, wielded ferociously, couldn't break a thing on the bike.

Most British and European motorcycle manufacturers adapted their machines to the American scene by changing details. Certain changes were obvious: Low European handlebars and kph speedometers gave way to higher "American" bars and mph instruments. The American marketplace automatically encouraged more-powerful versions of any given engine, or larger-displacement cousins. The American byword was power. When Triumph introduced its 650-cc Thunderbird to the United States, the 500-cc Speed Twin and Tiger 100's edged toward the background. Once a model was established in the American market, someone started to make "speed parts" for it. Higher compression ratios, hotter cams, more carburetion—that was the inevitable progression. In the land of straight roads and great distances, enthusiasts wanted strong engines and visceral motorcycles. American riders consciously traded away reliability, oil-tightness, dependable lights, and other details in order to get a fast motorcycle. The British understood that fact, delivered on it, and prospered by it.

In the case of America's most beloved single, the BSA Gold Star, engine development passed into American hands. Though other single-cylinder British motorcycles—such as Velocettes and Nortons—were not unknown in the United States, the BSA was probably the only single that American enthusiasts, as a body, really loved. Much of that passion related to the ease with which the Gold Star won American races in the early 1950's. The Gold Star was an all-round competition bike. Enduros, flat tracks, desert races, scrambles, trials—the big single was catholic in its abilities. In Europe, specialized machines, such as Manx Nortons in road racing and Husqvarnas in motocross, overshadowed the pushrod BSA, but in the United States, Gold Stars continued to be ridden on the road and raced successfully.

Indeed, the United States became the land of the strongest, fastest Gold Stars in the world, because American distributors and private tuners continued to develop the Gold Star for AMA flat-track and road racing. By the time the California speed tuners were finished, they had created engines which were BSA Gold Stars on the outside and Anglo-American hybrids on the inside. Even after the factory halted production of the single in 1963, Gold Stars were neither forgotten nor gone in America. The thumpers still droned around flat tracks, winning. Yankees were the last Gold Star loyalists.

It began as a ripple, running obliquely to the main current of things. Spontaneous and hidden, no one quite remembers the beginning, perhaps because there was no single beginning, but a number of them. Motorcycle dealers noticed it, some earlier, some later, but all by the mid- to late 1950's. It was, one dealer recalls, as if another person had walked into a room, unheard and unseen. One sensed a change but was unable to identify it immediately. Small motorcycles began selling, not briskly, but just selling. Import dealers perhaps stocked a couple of 175-cc or 250-cc NSU's to complement larger BMW's, or carried small Triumph Terriers or Cubs as part of their franchise agreement, or had lightweights on the showroom floor because someone at the dealership liked the bikes. Those 150- to 250-cc motorcycles disappeared from the showroom floors in the normal course of things. Dealers reordered. No big rush, no great startle, nothing more urgent than feeling a slight draft in a room and, without being too aware of it, closing an open window and going on about one's business. After all, anything under a 500-cc or

Honda's vertical-twin Super Hawk combined power and civility.

at the bottom a 350-cc, was hard to take seriously as a *real* motorcycle.

But then there was the Italian puzzle. Italian motorcycles began to sell after some importers, game enough to try, got the machines to their dealers. German lightweights were such competent, rational, civilized machines. But not those 100- to 200-cc Italian motorcycles. Although blessed with excellent engines and frames, there the blessings ended. The saddles were abusively hard. The paint faded into paler shades of blue or red on every exposure to bright sunny days. The mysteries of the electrical systems were outnumbered only by the irregular intervals at which the lights performed. Unlike the Ger-

man lightweights, which were unobtrusive, the Italian machines demanded that their owners love them if only to endure them. A 250-cc German motorcycle was a reasonable, affordable alternative to a larger machine. By comparison, a 175-cc Moto Parilla or Ducati just was not reasonable. Fun, yes; reasonable, no. More than anything else, the very fact that these motorcycles could succeed in the United States testified to the existence of an unknown number of motorcyclists who would buy into the sport, provided the right, or even not-so-right, lightweight motorcycles were offered. The motorcycle industry never consciously identified the new motorcyclists, but somehow the German lightweights simply stepped on them, while

The 305-cc engine was an amazing revelation to motorcyclists.

the Italian bikes managed to trip over them. Yet the steppers and trippers were not to be the movers and shakers; the Japanese were.

"You meet the nicest people on a Honda." From the start, there was an almost irresistible assumption that somehow this advertising slogan and campaign created the second coming of motorcycles in America. The slogan did no such thing. Fishing in an empty pool catches no fish. Words can't generate revolutions. Only social conditions can do that. Phrases may tap those resources and exploit conditions, but words do not make armies. Neither do they raise up markets. To say that advertising, however well done and pervasive, made motorcycling "socially re-

spectable" is to misunderstand the phenomenon.

Advertising, no matter how persuasively turned, can't succeed in a hostile environment. Had the Honda campaign been tried in the America of 1950, it would have shared the same fate as Ralph Rogers's "gentleman's motorcycle." The real question is not so much what Honda's advertising did, but what happened to the United States between 1950 and 1960.

Americans went into that critical sixth decade believing in a uniform and universal American way, and came out of the decade with that notion fairly shaken. Those who thought that the country was bolted together properly in 1949 wondered at its unscrewing by 1960. The

133

The CB-92 Honda Benly, a sporting 125-cc single-overhead-camshaft twin, had pressed-steel frame and forks. With giant brakes and five-figure revs, it was half street bike and half road racer. Many American riders campaigned race-kitted models.

United States accepted in shock the blow of Sputnik, fought a war it couldn't win, looked for domestic radicals who ultimately couldn't be found, and discovered minorities that insisted on their rights. By the end of the 1950's, everyone seemed less sure of his own answers and entertained the possibility of others. In 1950, the motorcyclist would be told that his motorcycle was dangerous and evil; in 1960 he would at least be asked if this were the case.

All this meant that challenges to loosening conformity could be made more easily. There was a tolerant receptivity to new things in America in 1960 that just had not been there in 1950. Honda's timing happened to be right, and the Japanese company's effort in the American market both encouraged and coincided with an increasing openness toward motorcycling.

Motorcycling's new social respectability emerged out of two interrelated factors. First, since Americans had this increasing openness toward previously taboo activities, even old-time motorcyclists, unchanged from 1950, were objects of a softer perception of motorcycling. Those who were nutballs in the public view of 1950 became far less so by 1960 standards. That was a kind of creeping social respectability through changing attitudes. Second, young members of the middle class bought into motorcycling. Social respectability for an activity is, in a sense, confirmed when socially respectable people engage in that activity. This kind of respectability also grows incrementally over a period of time: the more middle-class buyers, the more respectable the sport. Clearly, in the course of a decade the country had been changing, and so had motorcycling, and the second change would never have occurred without the first.

The real genius of Honda lay in its machines. While fishing an empty pool is hopeless, so is fishing with unbaited hooks. When Honda trolled, Americans bit. In the 1950's and more so in the 1960's, the American acqui-

sition game continued without let-up. Second cars met first ones inside double garages; two television sets were better than one; three telephones were an improvement over two. With this increasing affluence came an ability to test an activity by buying the necessary gear. Americans were so rich—or thought they were so rich—that they could try out a sport. It was a free-home-demonstration psychology, but the consumer paid for the goods. If he didn't like what he bought, he sold it, traded it, or sank it in a closet. Inside abundant America, little Hondas were an affordable experience. Americans bought, if not impulsively, then quickly. For $300 the new buyer could try motorcycling. It looked like fun, and it was worth the gamble.

Honda started rolling in the American market in 1959 with its minuscule "thrifty fifty," a step-through frame design with an enclosed 50-cc, four-stroke engine which would propel the device at about 40 or 45 mph. This Super Cub was a two-wheeled utility vehicle, aimed at a general transportation market rather than at motorcycle enthusiasts. Had Honda only offered the transporter, it would have created a short boom and then disappeared in a puff of memories. The 50-cc transportation market had no long-term future in the United States, where motorcycling had been a sport since the days of the Model T Ford. Honda also sold a genuine tiny motorcycle which, despite the 50-cc engine, had performance about equal to ordinary 125-cc motorcycles of the mid-1950's. The 50-cc tiddlers served to introduce thousands and thousands to two-wheeled sport. The introduction was easy because the motorcycles with tea-cup engines were so utterly disarming: small, light, dependable, oil-tight, quiet, and without temperament. The 50's did not give beginners a feeling that the machine might overwhelm them. Nor did the bikes look as if they would reply to a rider's error by smiting him. The machine said fun, not danger.

Very shortly, however, American riders discovered the limits of four-point-five horsepower motorcycling. The breathtaking aspect of 50-cc acceleration disappeared in about three days; then the bike seemed an absolute stone. Early on, one could be astounded that an engine displacing only 3 cubic inches would flash over 40 mph. A bit later, one wondered whether the motorcycle would ever nudge 50 mph. Those who really enjoyed motorcycling on a 50-cc machine planned to enjoy it more—just as soon as they bought a larger motorcycle.

Honda also made larger motorcycles. At the time, the 250 and 305 single-overhead-camshaft twins dominated the top of the line. These first "Dream" models looked strange to the American motorcyclist's eye: pressed-steel frames, stamped-out swinging arms, leading-link front forks, squarish headlights, deeply valanced fenders. There was nothing trim or stylish about them. If Western eyes did not like the way the Dream models looked, that could be remedied, too. Presto! Revised, more-powerful twin-cylinder engines appeared in entirely new motorcycles. Tubular frame and swinging arm, telescopic front forks, round headlight, narrow sports fenders—the list went on and on. The machines were the 250-cc Honda Hawk (CB-72) and the 305-cc Honda Super Hawk (CB-77). They were fresh, modern motorcycles.

The Super Hawk had all the things that Ralph Rogers would have wanted in a gentleman's motorcycle. The single-overhead-camshaft model was a vertical twin which produced peak power at 9,000 rpm. Honda's highly efficient engine put great performance in a very small package. The early Super Hawks would exceed a genuine 100 mph, and one usually had to go searching for motorcycles twice Honda's size before getting three-figure top speeds. The four-main-bearing lower end and overhead camshaft put the engine speeds a vast step above larger British vertical twins, which turned on two main bearings and moved valves with pushrods. Twin-cam brakes front

and rear set new standards for stopping inside the motorcycle world. Like the Speed Twin in its day, the Honda Super Hawk spoke performance.

Super Hawks had the civility of German machines and more. Electric starting had been designed into the engine; 12-volt electrics did justice to the Japanese reputation for electronics and wire-wizardry. Brilliant nighttime lights were taken for granted. The Super Hawk was a machine a rider could love because of things it did, not in spite of them. Around town, the Super Hawk stayed gentle on the ears, but above 6,000 rpm on the open road the mufflers sang a baleful howl as the engine rushed toward 9,000 rpm.

The chains of the past did not clank when the Japanese walked forward. The Japanese motorcycle manufacturers had such short histories that their attachment was to the present and the future in motorcycling. The Germans, who might have controlled the second coming of motorcycling in America, shifted their primary effort to automobiles by the mid-1950's. Harley-Davidson, witnessing the Indian debacle, knew the penalties for error. The Milwaukee company built machines it knew would sell and skirted bold experimentation. The British, faithful to vertical twins and singles, plodded forward. The Italians, content to meet one day at a time, faded.

The Japanese, however, wanted to build motorcycles, and modern ones, tailored to individual markets. The Honda Super Hawk shared much with motorcycling's past. It radiated machine quality and produced a telegraphic communication between machine and rider. The new social acceptance widened motorcycling's audience and opened another channel for the traditional American romance with machines. After all the clatter about social respectability and image, the baddies and the goodies, markets and slogans, the best thing about the revolution was the Honda Super Hawk.

8.

SUPERBIKES

The Japanese spoiled the quiet game of motorcycling in America. They dared to take it as a serious business. Before their arrival, the motorcycle industry was a slow-moving, low-pressure, hobby-store operation. From the end of World War II to 1960, the growth curve of the industry crawled upward gradually, comfortably, easily. BSA sold about 2,000 motorcycles on the East Coast of the United States in 1954, and 1954 was a pleasantly good year.

Every year dealers sold a few more machines. For the most part, they sold the same customers new machines every second or third year. In the northern states a dealer would sell most of his machines in the spring and early summer, repair and rebuild machines through the winter, and help organize hill climbs, road runs, scrambles, and other club events throughout the year. It was a friendly business. A dealer could get rapid delivery on parts, because the parts—as well as the motorcycles—didn't change very much from year to year. Everyone, it seemed, was on a first-name basis with everyone else: factory executive to dealer, dealer to customer, customer to mechanic. The coffeepot perked unceasingly, because motorcycle shops were good places to sip coffee and kill time. Friday and Saturday nights motorcyclists stopped by to catch up on the news: who had just bought what machine from whom, what troubles someone was having with his bike, who had won some distant flat-track race, when the new saddlebags and high-compression pistons would be in stock, and how much faster someone's bike became with the addition of a "three-quarters-race" camshaft. It was a small, clubby, out-of-the-way sport.

Machines didn't change drastically, but there were developments. Triumph introduced a 650 in 1950. Plunger frames and hardtails gave way to swinging-arm frames. In 1957 Harley-Davidson showed its 55-cu. in. Sportster with overhead valves—and that caused quite a splash, following as it did just a few years after the intro-

duction of the new side-valve 45-cu. in. and 55-cu. in. V-twins. No one could ever accuse the motorcycle industry of beating into the future at a frantic pace. The motorcycle magazines carried advertisements from manufacturers and importers which invited the reader to make his hobby his business and become a motorcycle dealer. After all, hadn't everyone else?

The Japanese were truly in the motorcycle business, unencumbered by history and Friday-night coffee gatherings. The British, American, and German motorcycle industries were generally content with the pleasant world as they found it. Not so the Japanese. Where others saw problems, the Japanese saw opportunities. While others might think about all the reasons why something couldn't be built, the Japanese were considering how easily something could be cast, machined, and assembled. Their new products began attracting more and more American enthusiasts. Honda's Super Hawk taught the Japanese an important lesson about performance: Americans bought packaged speed and power. Motorcycling's Old Guard manufacturers in America had long known this fact but had acted slowly on the knowledge, gradually tuning up their bigger models and occasionally introducing something new. True, the Japanese in 1960 were far from building the highest-performance motorcycle in the world; as quick and fast as the Super Hawk ran, its performance was a long step away from matching the strongest machines on the road.

American motorcycle riders never got bogged down in hairsplitting definitions of performance. Everyone knew what a fast motorcycle was and what it did. A fast motorcycle sat at the last stoplight in town, waiting for the green; and when it came, a fast motorcycle would rocket away on a thunderclap of noise and reach any point along the two-lane blacktop quicker than anything else in town. And, if need be, it would give the slip on top-end to any vehicle around. That was superbike performance, American-style—simple and brutal.

British and continental motorcycle enthusiasts could not quite comprehend the attraction straight-line contests held for Americans. Surely, they believed, the handling and braking qualities so important to the sporting motorcycle in England and Europe figured into the American conception of performance. Not so; American roads were as straight as foreign roads were crooked. Only gradually did Americans begin to appreciate the quantitative and qualitative differences in handling and braking from one machine to another. One might arc gracefully through a corner in little chattering slips, and another might corner (faster or slower) in a series of frightening lurches and heaves. Brakes could be weak or powerful, smooth or grabby at the extremes. Most American enthusiasts weren't interested in this sort of "European performance." Only in the 1960's, when the differences in handling and braking between old and new motorcycles became pronounced, did American enthusiasts begin to understand that measurable performance extended to braking and handling.

Performance on Mainstreet U.S.A. in 1955 centered on engines. No one ever held stopping contests, and in most point-to-point chases, a fast engine was the determining factor. Straight-line confrontations had a certain directness. The long burns down the road compressed to a minimum the differences in riding skill, making any dispute a contest between motorcycles rather than riders. With the burn-ups came a natural escalation. Engines grew in displacement. After they reached their natural or unnatural displacement limits, the engines—modified more and more—displayed unwelcome consequences: They were fussy, shaky, and fragile. Edward Turner's Speed Twin design suffered. The motorcycle had started out as a relatively smooth, silent, flexible device which would hum along at 70 or 75 mph and chase up near the century mark. By comparison, later Tiger 100's were less smooth, quiet, and flexible, though more powerful than Turner's first effort. The Triumph crankshaft assembly had only main-bearing support at the outboard ends and no support between the cylinders. Once the lower end was strengthened to deal with the increasing power output, the crankshaft no longer flexed, but the 500 engine began vibrating.

The larger the British vertical-twin engines became—the more reciprocating mass they possessed—the more the engines shook. High-compression pistons and elevated crankshaft speeds had deleterious effects on crankshaft assemblies without center main-bearing support. By the mid-1960's, the big British vertical twins weren't known as British Shaker Twins for nothing. The 750 Norton Atlas, which may have set a high mark for vibration, shook with such dreadful enthusiasm that it was almost enough to detach riders' hands at the wrists, or perhaps the elbows. Passing scenery went to a blur—not from the speed but from the shaking. Those 750 Nortons possessed dazzling speed if the rider could withstand the vibration long enough to enjoy the horsepower. The shaking attacked the motorcycle as well as the rider, so that the machine was constantly undergoing self-destructive disassembly. What didn't vibrate off in a spray of nuts and bolts might break. The model had an unenviable record for reliability. Those tightly strung British vertical twins had performance, at a price. Americans were still willing to pay, but not for very much longer.

These things the Japanese observed. Building fast motorcycles was easy for them, since Japan almost alone was building modern motorcycle engines. New engines which sprang from new blueprints produced more power; inherent difficulties of old designs didn't exist for the Japanese, since they had no old designs.

141

British machinery evolved piecemeal.
Above: The Norton vertical twin,
which grew over the years from a 500 to
an 850, came to rest in the
Commando chassis with Isolastic engine
mounts. Right: The Triumph
Trident honored the past with its
classic Triumph looks and
its 750-cc three-cylinder engine.

Nowhere did the Japanese demonstrate their expertise more than with the development of two-stroke engines. Traditionally, if a manufacturer had wanted to make a cheap engine, he built a two-stroke, which had fewer moving parts, required the mixing of oil and gasoline, performed fair to poorly, emitted a blue oil haze from the exhausts, and seized pistons at regular, unhappy intervals. With few exceptions, two-strokes were regarded with disdain in the United States. By the early 1960's, the Japanese utilized new technology to build vastly superior two-stroke engines. Oil injection eliminated the mixing chore and gave more accurate lubrication. New materials and construction methods improved cylinder sealing and diminished seizure prospects. Updates in cylinder porting and scavenging increased performance. Yamaha, Suzuki, and Kawasaki weren't alone in developing this two-stroke technology, but they did have the most sophisticated engines available to the motorcycling public.

Kawasaki, a latecomer to the American scene, reaffirmed the old formula for creating a stir: build fast motorcycles. Although the company's 250-cc and 350-cc two-stroke twins weren't sluggards, Kawasaki unveiled the purest expression of horsepower salesmanship anyone had ever seen in America: a 500-cc, three-cylinder, two-stroke speedster. The motorcycle was astonishingly fast. From a standing start, well-tuned models could clear a quarter-mile in under 13 seconds at speeds beyond 100 mph. A top speed around 125 mph was no idle claim. In 1969, there wasn't another 500 or 650 that could get within sniffing distance of the Kawasaki three. The motorcycle lacked inspired handling; when ridden fast down a bumpy, winding road the first Kawasaki 500 triples were positively scary. And at the last stoplight in town, counting toward the green light, the 500 Kawasaki was best treated with respect and skill, for more than one insensitive fool was taken on a wild, hopping, half-motorcycle, half-unicycle, nerve-sizzling ride when the light turned green. American enthusiasts loved it, and bought the motorcycle for that shot-from-a-cannon feeling.

Cannon shots aside, there was another significant thing about the Kawasaki 500: It was a business motorcycle. The machine was the product of a calculated, tough-minded business approach to the American market. It did not develop accidentally, nor was it built to meet motoring needs in Japan. Kawasaki tailored the machine to American tastes.

The first production models of high-performance Japanese motorcycles were also the most powerful, and that fact also bore some business importance. The traditional non-Japanese order of things called for a standard model to be introduced one year, followed by a "tuned" sports version within a couple of years. The Japanese reasoned that the power-conscious Yankees should receive the strongest version first, thus maximizing the impact of the new machine. Later, after two years or so, the motorcycle might undergo a subtraction of horsepower. The model numbers remained the same, so there was never officially a new "lower-performance" version. Rather, the original model, thanks to internal tuning changes, grew softer.

There were few technical terrors bred into the new *macht-schnell* motorcycles. The Japanese had the engineering variables so securely under their control by the mid-1960's that they could manufacture a tuned version of a new motorcycle from the beginning without stumbling over the unreliability line. In the old fast-motor-later system, the degree of tuning the standard model could withstand had to be determined experimentally by factory testers, in accordance with the old break-it-and-fix-it procedure. The fiddling and testing could delay the sports version a year or two. The Japanese simply calculated by computer and slide rule what old-time manufacturers tried to determine in the field. Finally, the Japanese didn't need to stagger their performance models, because they usually had new, larger, stronger motorcycles waiting to be put on stage. Busy competing with one another, the Japanese walked out new models at a furious clip. Thus, the 500-cc Kawasaki three-cylinder two-stroke underwent de-tuning in 1971, as Kawasaki rolled out its final version of cannon-shot motorcycling.

The Kawasaki 750, another three-cylinder, two-stroke machine, had performance so devastating that it could humble all other motorcycles. Neither comfortable nor graceful in cornering, the 750 Kawasaki could still best other machines point-to-point over winding roads, thanks to its tremendous accelerative and decelerative capabilities. The 750 Kawasaki represented the end point of hot-rod motorcycles. Americans still loved straight-line performance, but most enthusiasts also wanted civility. The 750 Kawasaki proved itself a noisy, vibrating gas guzzler, and that left it outside the mainstream of motorcycle development, which had shifted away from one-dimensional performance machines. A raw, visceral performer just was not enough.

There was another kind of machine—powerful, sophisticated, and detailed—a balanced, civil package which marked the central channel of big-motorcycle development: the Honda 750 Four. Introduced in 1969, there had never been anything like it before. It was a logical motorcycle without peer. There was no real way to develop a high-performance motorcycle without using a big engine, and a big engine traditionally meant a lot of vibration. The most reasonable and straightforward engineering solution for Honda was a smooth-running multicylinder design, specifically a four-cylinder, four-stroke, single-overhead-camshaft engine. Designing and building a four-cylinder motorcycle engine presented no impassable barriers to Honda; the engineering technology for such an engine had existed for some time, and the manufacturer had the necessary resources to build modern engines.

A four-cylinder motorcycle carried a weight debit, but also a potential horsepower credit. Those small reciprocating parts that minimized vibration could also be made to go up and down a lot faster than in a comparable twin-cylinder design. By pumping more gas and air together, turning more revolutions inside any given minute, the four-cylinder engine could produce more power. For Honda, then, there was no witchcraft whatever to building a four-cylinder engine. It was all in a normal business day of engineering and production.

If the 750-cc, four-cylinder motorcycle was going to be fast and heavy, then it needed excellent brakes. Honda created a hydraulic front disc brake for the 750 Four which became the standard by which to judge other brakes. In 1969 the Honda disc outstopped everything else —and the braking pressure rose in direct proportion to hand-lever pressure, something that did not happen with drum brakes. In the hierarchy of things difficult, creating a disc brake for a motorcycle is not near the top. It wasn't as if disc brakes were unknown, but in the myopic motorcycle industry, no one had ever used a hydraulic disc brake on a genuinely mass-produced motorcycle. Given the knowledge about the superiority of disc brakes in the automotive field, sooner or later the speed and weight of big motorcycles would force a switch to discs. While everyone else in the motorcycle business asked, "Why not later?" Honda asked, "Why not now?"

All kinds of reasons for success go on parade when examining the Japanese motorcycle industry. The first holds that Japanese companies are huge and enjoy great economies of scale. Then the frayed cheap-labor thesis is trotted out. Other Western apologists point to the competitive nature of the Japanese. And, as all Westerners know, the Japanese government encourages Japa-

For many Americans no machine ever equaled the Harley-Davidson Sportster's brutish, visceral charm, although Kawasaki's two-stroke three-cylinder 750 (above), easily outclassed the Sportster as a gunshot motorcycle. Left: The Honda 750 Four demonstrated that performance and ultrarefinement could be blended together.

nese industry in many ways. And so on. All this talk about the Japanese motorcycle industry assumes that the Japanese did something highly unusual. Which, of course, they did—compared to that traditional hobby-operation that called itself the motorcycle industry in Western countries. The Old Guard manufacturers never took the business of manufacturing motorcycles seriously. The Japanese did. In a sense they were passionless about manufacturing motorcycles. They proceeded with the same kind of logic that most large corporations employ when building pots and pans, television sets, dishwashers, heavy equipment, and automobiles. If a market situation called for electric starters or four-cylinder machines, the Japanese simply went ahead and designed them. Such was their business-like approach to motorcycles.

There can be little doubt that the Japanese happened upon the American market just at the time when social, economic, and cultural conditions could generate a huge number of potential motorcycle enthusiasts. It wasn't necessary for any maker to have a panoramic view of the nature of the American market. It was enough to have the basic, narrowly focused business vision to produce what a market was buying. No one had to draw a picture for Kawasaki or Honda to know that machines like the 500-cc Kawasaki triple or the Honda 750-cc four-cylinder would sell. British and American and most European manufacturers likewise knew that, but an unwillingness to act damped out any mid-1960's response. That same unwillingness to act, that reluctance to take motorcycling seriously, hindered anyone outside the Japanese from tapping the small-motorcycle field. The old-school mentality thought that 50-cc and 90-cc motorcycles were not really proper machines. Then the Japanese turned out fresh designs in the 125-cc to 250-cc categories. Still the old-school sports waited, expecting that the boom would finally reach their pet displacement classes—500 cc

and up, the "legitimate" field of motorcycling. Meanwhile, they said, let the Japanese motorcycle industry go on helping everyone to bigger sales—which, indeed, it was doing. In this way, they betrayed their distrust of motorcycling as legitimate business. The Old Guard was just along for the ride, trying to contribute the minimum and extract the maximum from the sport and with nearly the same old motorcycles. That was 1964.

The Japanese brought the old-school club, kicking and screaming, into the 1970's. The builders of big, fast motorcycles finally had to react to Honda and Kawasaki. It was no longer enough to make developments of developments and refinements of developments of past designs. Only the British, with their conservative creativity, steered that course with any success.

The Norton Commando was the finest example of British creativity. The Norton name, a fixture in British motorcycling, limped out of the corporate collapse of Associated Motor Cycles and into the Norton-Villiers combine. There the venerable engine was rescued from the old Norton and Matchless frames, and dropped into a new one, to form the new Commando model. The brilliant frame of the Norton Commando was probably the only one in motorcycling that ever salvaged an engine. The Norton 750 vertical-twin had shaken and vibrated mightily in its old framework; the Commando frame isolated the shaker twin by mounting it in rubber. The engine was canted forward fifteen degrees, bolted to the separate transmission with a pair of steel plates which also carried the pivot for the rear swinging arm. This whole sub-assembly was rubber-mounted to the main frame by means of Silentbloc shock mounts. By all that was known, or thought to be known, this system should have wrecked the motorcycle's handling. After all, one could move the rear wheel laterally, relative to the main frame, by hand. Such slop between the swing-arm pivot and the steering neck theoretically should have planted the rider in the bushes at the first curve. Only it didn't work that way. Confounding all naysayers, who thought the frame would bury the Norton name along with the first few Commando riders, the motorcycle proved a good steerer. Most important, the frame allowed the rider to escape the engine vibrations which poisoned the old Atlas. So there it rested: a magnificent frame to save an overaged engine. The Japanese would never have bothered with the innovation. As hard-nosed engineers, they dealt with problems at their source. The Japanese would have discarded the Norton engine in an instant. The British adapted.

The old engine received another update in an effort to yank and shove it toward the 1970's. Among other things, it got a new clutch, since the old item had never been designed to cope with a 750-cc engine. A five-speed gearbox would have been a welcome improvement, but the gearbox shell did not lend itself to an expansion to five speeds. The Norton engine itself belonged to an earlier technology. The Commando version, while improved in details and quality control, reached a natural limit. The Norton Commando S was as fast as it would ever effectively be, despite the enlargement to 850 cc later on.

The 750 Norton Commando was an amazing motorcycle. By 1969 it was in the same speed league with Japanese multicylinder motorcycles. A swift Commando wheeling down a mountain road could charm a rider and lull him into a fit of forgetfulness. He could forget that he kicked the motorcycle to life, forget that only four speeds lived in the gearbox, forget that oil-tightness was still not an English virtue, forget that the engine belonged to the 1950's. If the old school had any genius, it lay in beguiling riders into such fits.

When given a new engine to design, the British, in particular the Birmingham Small Arms company in the late 1960's, could not or would not break with the past.

Norton, which rushed out the Commando just before multicylinder motorcycles began appearing, might be excused—in the name of survival—for sticking with Bert Hopwood's engine and the past; Norton had to do something, and quick, just to continue making motorcycles. On the other hand, BSA started fresh. Building a new 750 engine presented British motorcycling with the greatest engineering opportunity of a generation or two. From scratch, there was a chance to do a whole new engine. When the 750 emerged, it looked suspiciously as if BSA had at first decided to build a 750-cc, three-cylinder, four-stroke engine by cutting an old Speed Twin in half and sandwiching in a third cylinder—using old parts in a "new" engine—but had then shifted concepts at midpoint and decided to make the 750 engine a thing unto itself.

Where was the electric starter? Where was the five-speed gearbox? BSA succeeded in building a completely new unit in the late 1960's, and when it had finished, the new engine had no more speeds in the gearbox than the twenty-year-old Norton design. The transmission itself was something of a wonder. The power input into the transmission and the exit from it followed a perplexing route. The arrangement demanded that one dismantle the engine primary and clutch, or the gearbox, just to change an engine output sprocket. This inconvenience allowed the British to use some existing gearbox parts, but more than anything else, the gearbox ins-and-outs suggested that the engine was built first as a toolroom exercise, and later designed. The engine impressed the studious onlooker as pure development, as something that talented mechanics might piece together using parts off the stock shelves.

It was that pure development quality that made British motorcycles, such as the BSA-Triumph 750, appear to be products of gifted hobbyists, from top to bottom. One could imagine the whole scenario: A group of

Any Superbike contains a series of trade-offs. Add ride-comfort, for example, and subtract handling. Sporting Ducati motorcycles, sohc V-twins, are spare, functional machines. Right: The 750 Sport has a valve-spring engine. Below: Super Sport has desmodromic valve actuation; the valves are opened and closed mechanically by rocker arms. Both superb steerers, the Sport can do 125 mph with its 8,000-rpm engine; the Desmo can go 140-mph-plus, 9,500 rpm.

nearsighted or no-sighted hobby-store executives find their company confronted with significant competition. Wanting something done quickly, the hobby managers assign a group of talented mechanics the task of assembling a new hobbyhorse. The mechanics, who may have built an experimental hobbyhorse once upon a time just for fun, drag out the pieces and screw a new horse together. The new horse is pure development.

The British may possess a knack for development unknown elsewhere. The British could take two perfectly straight boards and develop them incrementally into rockers, while the Japanese would design and cast rockers in aluminum in the first place. The cast rockers are taken for granted, while one is always amazed that the fiddled boards work at all. On paper, the Trident shouldn't have been a more powerful engine than the four-cylinder Honda, but the Triumph was. On verbal recitation of the basic specifications, the Trident was a less complicated engine mechanically than the Japanese four. Yet such a recitation concealed the complexity of the British triple's primary-clutch-and-transmission system, which made the Honda's

drive train look simple indeed. In one respect, the three-cylinder BSA-Triumph engine was very much like Norton's Commando frame. By all rights neither one should have worked too well. But they both did.

Development continued on the British machines. When the Commando and Triumph Trident were announced, they sported drum brakes, which the Honda 750 disc system immediately made obsolete. And so the British went through the trouble and expense of building two brake systems—drum and disc—instead of one. Development surely wasn't as exciting as the Japanese way, where the new product was finished upon introduction.

Development or no, going into the 1970's, the members of the old club were just about where they had started. They were building motorcycles for a relatively small, enthusiastic clientele who understood the peculiarities and eccentricities of particular motorcycles. If the motorcycle leaked oil, well, you had to understand that British motorcycles leaked a little motor oil. If the motorcycle proved a stubborn and snappish starter, well, you had to understand that a gas-flooded Harley-Davidson

Sportster would not kickstart easily. There was a difference, though. In the early 1960's, the old-school club constituted the big-sports-bike universe. By the early 1970's, they were a raft floating in a modern sea of machines engineered and built in Japan.

The old club stayed afloat because the raft was the last preserve for traditionalists. Norton and Triumph wanted "new" written all over their 750's. They resorted to stylized newness. The Norton Commando flaunted a fiberglass tail section on its seat, and the Triumph Trident carried ray-gun mufflers and a creased-and-kneaded breadloaf gas tank. American customers raised eyebrows at Norton's tailpiece (which eventually disappeared in the United States), and Triumph's American clientele would not accept the Flash Gordon getup on the new three-cylinder. Americans refused to buy the Halloween-look Triumph. In the Triumph customer's eyes, the new 750 triple had to look like a Triumph; the present had to fit with the past. If the motorcycle had been entirely fresh, the Trident might have uncovered a new following with no ties to tradition. That never happened. Fundamentally, the Trident was a conservative machine which appealed to conservative motorcyclists. Very quickly, the Trident assumed the classic Triumph look.

One body of motorcyclists wanted motorcycles that shouted "classic machine"; they regarded Japanese motorcycles as too slick, too refined, too civilized. For them the old bits-and-pieces British approach had an attraction; one could grasp how a component was literally pieced together. Black boxes, always inviolate on Japanese motorcycles, would open to tinkering on British motorcycles. The Japanese machines, the traditionalists argued, were too indivisible to love. Given the chance, the traditionalist might construct a motorcycle in the same way as British factories. The garden-shed tinkerer could see the wisdom of Triumph's using an automobile clutch in a three-cylinder motorcycle. The Mini-Cooper's clutch could be made to work, so why not use it? It was the outlook of an assembler, as differentiated from a designer. The psychic distance between those who built British motorcycles and those who bought them was short.

Harley-Davidson had an advantage over British industry. The Milwaukee firm already had a monster engine for its roadburner. The Harley-Davidson Sportster packed a 55-cu. in. overhead-valve engine, and that engine had made the Harley-Davidson model the first superbike in the simple, narrow American definition. Introduced in 1957, the Sportster had reigned for years at the last stoplight in town. Engines were the very center of performance motorcycles, and in the matter of size the Harley-Davidson was very generously endowed. The company understood much about American motorcycling, especially that straight-line performance was one of the principal attractions of motorcycles. A big engine would propel a motorcycle fast for a long period of time in the United States, and a narrow-angle V-twin was a good way to get a big engine into a relatively small space. These were lessons from the past, increasingly dated by new motorcycle technology. Yet Harley-Davidson knew that motorcycling was an emotional, subjective experience—and the look of the Harley-Davidson Sportster was right. The engine dominated the whole machine, balanced on both ends by the large forms of the wheels, and capped by a small gas tank. It was elegant and simple. The motorcycle exuded a machine-like quality. There was an aural attraction, too. The V-twin's staggered combustion pulses gave the Sportster a distinctive beat out of the exhaust pipes. The motorcycle was tall, skinny, crude, raucous, and fast in a straight line. Though Harley-Davidson investigated other layouts over the years, inertia or wisdom or both kept the V-twins coming out of Milwaukee. In any event, the Sportster was a cultist's machine. That was understandable. In the

United States, motorcycling had been a small, out-of-the-way sport for forty years, and Harley-Davidson belonged emotionally to the old-school club. Milwaukee could not go head-to-head with the Japanese.

More than any other machine, the big Harley-Davidson increasingly relied on its machine charisma. Though the engine grew to one litre, civilizing touches such as quiet mufflers blunted the old sting. The enormous V-twin still had the horsepower that further development could pull out of it, and in this respect the Sportster was better off than Norton's Commando. Yet a problem lingered. The Sportster traditionally could do one thing well: out-accelerate and out-run almost anything. By 1969 the American twin was ex-champion in that category, and by the early 1970's it was just an also-ran.

In some ways, Harley-Davidson labored under handicaps. Like the British, it lived out of the knapsack of other industries. The domestic American carburetors, which were not designed for motorcycle application but which Milwaukee wanted to use, were crude and outdated. Some progress there was. At least, with the addition of a disc brake up front, the Sportster stopped better. Though not unlike British-style development, Harley-Davidson's brand of old-school behavior seemed less hidebound. The Milwaukee company had expanded into Italy, buying Aermacchi in 1960, and it imported small Italian motorcycles built to American specifications. And no one in Milwaukee talked about developing the V-twin Sportster over a period of twenty years, or about the charisma of the big V-twin never fading. Machines like the 903-cc Kawasaki Z-1 guaranteed change.

Kawasaki found a way of combining the civility which most American enthusiasts wanted in a motorcycle with the performance which most riders believed they wanted—if only to say that it was on tap. Kawasaki created a big sports motorcycle which could nearly be all things to all riders, a kind of latter-day Honda 750 Four. For those riders who dismissed Nortons, Triumphs, and Harley-Davidsons as relics of the past, the Kawasaki 903-cc four-cylinder motorcycle offered electric starting, a full count of warning lights, solid electrics, conveniently integrated hand switches, reasonable pedal and lever pressures, and so on. The Kawasaki had all those convenience features, all those marks of civility that most enthusiasts expected from modern machines, and none of the noise, temperament, and nickel-rocket commotion which the Kawasaki three-cylinder, two-stroke motorcycle—or any other unregenerate superbike—radiated. One could get off a Honda, Suzuki, or Yamaha, get on the big Kawasaki, ride mile after mile and, without tweaking the throttle too hard, believe one was aboard another rational, civilized, logical product from the Orient. Which, of course, he certainly would be.

For those who love machinery, the Kawasaki 903 was the first double-overhead-camshaft, four-cylinder, mass-produced motorcycle. Granted, hardware lovers who had a passion for the bits-and-pieces approach might find the Kawasaki a little indivisible and homogenized, but the engine was a twin-cam design which scored with lovers of nuts and bolts. For those who demanded the excitement of high performance in a straight line, sending the big Kawasaki's tachometer needle toward the red zone and shifting gears would squeeze wide-open spaces at a rate most riders had never before experienced. It left them thankful the machine had no evil intent in its handling and used a disc brake for stopping. The time had passed when a new motorcycle could exhibit incompetent brakes or foul handling on winding roads, and have such faults go unnoticed or excused. Enthusiasts could be concerned about more than just engines, since the engines were becoming more and more unobtrusive. Civilized motorcycles, because they lacked the temperament, noise, and general

Top: The Kawasaki Z-1, with its powerful four-cylinder dohc 900-cc engine, insures that Japanese civility will never become dull. Above: Equally well-mannered and more luxurious than any other motorcycle available is the BMW R90S, a 900-cc flat twin. Bottom: Laverda's 750 vertical twin lacks the one-litre model's raw horsepower.

rowdiness of rougher-hewn machines, could almost seem dull and appliance-like in comparison.

The civilizing process by definition had to separate the rider from all the thrashing going on inside the engine and elsewhere on the motorcycle. Silent, smooth, well-mannered, low-powered motorcycles faintly smelled of drabness. But not the Kawasaki 903-cc four-cylinder. A machine which would clear a quarter-mile in 12.5 seconds from a standing start at well beyond 100 mph—and do it easily—could not be dull. A motorcycle which could maintain 120 mph cruising speed without gasping in the least just could not be a drab machine. The Kawasaki's sheer engine performance, delivered with the grace and power of a velvet bludgeon, removed any creeping tedium that civilization had put into the motorcycle. Its performance was calculated to keep excitement at a high level while smoothing out all the rough crests. The Japanese took desires for ultraperformance and civility seriously. That was their business. It was cold logic, not love, that produced a machine such as the 903-cc Kawasaki Z-1. Love was the bailiwick of the old-school hobbyists. Love and Old World craftsmanship were poor business.

The Italians shrugged off business. They had to be collared into the American market, and they demonstrated a talent for building what they wanted to build, despite all attempts to suggest what the American market might require. That, from time to time, the Italian effort in America almost died is a matter of record. That such a demise would not have concerned the Italians is also a matter of truth. Italians manufactured what they wanted, for themselves. If anyone else liked what they built, he could buy it. If not, the Italians shrugged.

Moto Guzzi proved steadier on the American scene than most Latins, selling a brutish, shaft-drive motorcycle powered by a transverse V-twin engine which grew in stages from 700 to 850 cc. The motorcycle was a big, trucky touring machine without merit as a real superbike. But in 1971 Moto Guzzi stuffed its gigantic engine-and-transmission package into a low, compact frame. The result was a 750-cc sports machine which handled beautifully, and rode in comfort, thanks to its supple suspension. The engine shook the bike sideways below 3,500 rpm, but above that figure the vibration mellowed and faded. With its electric starter, shaft drive, and careful (for Italians) quality control, the Moto Guzzi Sport came as close to the packaged sophistication of Japanese bikes as any Italian motorcycle. Yet, unlike the big Japanese and British machines, the development of the Moto Guzzi Sport had nothing to do with the American market. The motorcycle was one expression of the European conception of high-speed grand touring. Far from being built with American superhighways in mind, the Guzzi Sport was bred for fast continental riding, which included bursts up the Autostrada and charges down narrow roads which snaked over and around mountain ranges. These conditions demanded more than straight power. They required superior handling and first-class braking.

The sporting Italian motorcycles aimed at the Lamborghini class of motorcycle riders in Europe, where big, fast, sporting motorcycles enjoyed a revival in the 1970's. During the 1950's and early 1960's, in Italy and elsewhere in Europe, the transportation market for two-wheelers, aside from mopeds, gradually fell apart, as small Fiats, Volkswagens, and Renaults put roofs over drivers and passengers. This change, for example, led NSU away from motorcycles and into automobiles. In Great Britain, of course, the collapse of the domestic motorcycle transportation market only reinforced the British dependence on the American sports trade. The Italians, who had concentrated on small motorcycles and constantly trod the edge of bankruptcy, lost some manufacturers during the lean years, but generally managed to struggle through.

The sporting motorcyclist, whether riding a 175-cc speedster in Italy or a fast British twin in France, almost but never quite disappeared in Europe. Rising affluence, which had erased the motorcycles as transportation, later fostered the European upswing in sport cycling. A genuine enthusiasts' market, not unlike the American scene, emerged. The glamour machines—500-cc-and-up sports motorcycles—had performance far beyond the boldest pretensions of any Fiat. Expensive motorcycles like the Moto Guzzi Sport were perfect instruments for high-speed, high-visibility motoring. These motorcycles were not two-wheeled substitutes for Ferraris and Lamborghinis, they were European motorcycling's equivalent to such automobiles.

One could not forget that Italian roadburners had their roots elsewhere. Guzzi Sports, as well as MV Agusta 750's and Ducati 750 Sports and Super Sports, had no air cleaners fitted; that was just the Italian way. The German high-powered grand-touring machines were better detailed. BMW had always been in the touring side of the motorcycling spectrum. While the German company had built some early "sports" models, such as the R69S and R50S, it had never stepped squarely into the performance business. A good Harley-Davidson Sportster or Norton Atlas could mow down a BMW in any contest of pure speed in a short sprint.

BMW had such solid, dependable motorcycles —and an automobile business—that the company went along for years without substantially altering its motorcycles. As good touring machines tend to be, they were civilized devices: smooth, comfortable, reliable, and slow. When, in 1969, BMW built totally new, horizontally opposed twins, they were moving their motorcycles toward sports machinery at just about the time sports machinery was shifting toward traditional BMW virtues of motorcycle civility. BMW always believed that a motorcycle should be just as reliable and easy to keep as an automobile. Among other things, this point of view led to shaft-driven, smooth-running, opposed twins, and to moderate outputs for any given engine displacement. Although the Japanese went after a high reliability factor with different engineering formats, the big Japanese machines, such as the Kawasaki 903 and Honda 750 four-cylinder motorcycles, delivered automotive-type dependability, which earlier had been the preserve of German machinery.

The redesigned BMW R75/5 illustrated this narrowing of the sports/civility gap; the 1969 model occupied a middle ground between genuine touring machines and the high-performance superbikes. On the German side, the gap disappeared entirely when the BMW R90S rolled out of West Germany with a powerful 900-cc engine, five-speed gearbox, double-disc brakes, electric starter, and full instrumentation. The touring heritage meant that the BMW did not lack air cleaners—or any other equipment that would stamp the bike as the product of a special geographic area. The very fact that BMW built a heavy sporting motorcycle testified to the renewed growth of the sports-motorcycle market in Germany and Europe at large, and in the United States.

One final piece of evidence indicated how times had changed. As BMW announced their new R90 series, the company terminated the 500-cc twin, their basic pedestrian transportation machine. The factory observed that it "is not included in the range of BMW machines any more, as purchasers and enthusiasts today show a much greater interest in the category of very powerful bikes."

BMW managed with two cylinders what Kawasaki had put into four. Moto Laverda in Italy opted for three cylinders, double-overhead camshafts and 1,000 cc. Like the Moto Guzzi Sport, the Laverda 1000 had its origin in European conditions rather than in the American market. Indeed, Laverda had a minimal interest in the United

States, and a near-zero enthusiasm for export to North America. Short-coupled and stout, almost stubby in appearance, the one-litre motorcycle could peel scenery past the rider with alarming rapidity and majestic serenity. It possessed the same kind of performance and ease which blessed the Kawasaki 903. Large instruments—tachometer and speedometer—would be familiar to the first-time Laverda rider, who would note the instruments came from the same maker that supplies Honda.

Perhaps the instruments carry a lesson. Motorcycling has experienced internationalization, as Europeans begin to shop in the Japanese emporium for suppliers. There is a coming-together, and the Laverda 1000 suggests an eventual melding of superbike concepts.

Stifling conformity will not likely descend upon motorcycling. Consider the Ducati 750, which embraces both the past *and* rational design. Basically, the 750-cc unit is two single-overhead-camshaft Ducati singles joined in a ninety-degree V-twin engine. That description is a bit too bald. More precisely, the 750 engine is closely patterned on the earlier, smaller single, and both engines share the same engineering traditions and working technology. A reliance on tradition does not necessarily imply backward, irrational engineering. Indeed, the Ducati 750 is an extreme example of form following function. Ducati wanted a smooth-running twin-cylinder engine; that dictated a ninety-degree V-twin configuration, which has perfect primary balance and a rocking couple occurring at twice crankshaft speed. The net result was a lack of any vibration without resort to rubber insulation or antivibration systems designed into the engine.

No one but Italians would have built such a thing. The Japanese would sense, correctly, that the motorcycle would simply look too peculiar to sell in substantial (Japanese) numbers. Thus, when Yamaha decided to build a four-stroke twin, they elected to construct a traditional vertical twin and control the vibration with two counter-rotating weights moving in the opposite direction of the crankshaft. Besides, the Ducati 750 engine, chock full of gears (four sets of helical-cut bevel gears just to run the camshafts), would prove expensive to build anywhere. But Ducati wasn't much interested in looks, or markets, or business as spoken in Japan. Only a small maker could get away with such a design, which is to say that Ducati, as well as Laverda and Moto Guzzi, had become the newest and most creative members of the old-school club.

Superbikes have never been so splendiferous, so different, so plentiful. In the early 1970's, the superbike shopper could opt for a boisterous one-dimensional performer, the Kawasaki 750 three-cylinder two-stroke, which inherited its cannon-shot title from Harley-Davidson's Sportster. The American V-twin, even with cooled performance, had lost little of its spellbinding charisma. Did the enthusiast love the British bits-and-pieces approach to fast motorcycling? The Norton Commando demonstrated that England was still the home of the creative conservative, and the Triumph 750 three-cylinder Trident stood as a tribute to British development engineering.

Was it civility and performance that the shopper craved? Then he could select a balance between handling, braking, and acceleration—and civility—by choosing carefully: Honda's 750 Four, Kawasaki's twin-cam 903, BMW's R90 series, Moto Guzzi's Sport.

Did the Italian notion of high-performance motorcycling touch the enthusiast's soul? Laverda provided a high-intensity one-litre solution and Ducati a stark, functional *tour de force*.

Whatever the choice, the superbike would make the rider a true believer. And he would know: However cold one manufacturer's engineering figures might be, or how warm another maker's traditions might remain—buying a superbike was truly an act of passion.

OFF-ROAD EXPLOSION

Jack Hoel had an inquiring mind. It was only natural that he wondered how Dave Holeman battered himself on weekends. Holeman would come to work on Monday mornings with the landing sides of his forearms bruised and his elbows neatly rounded off.

Hoel was also a man paid to wonder. In charge of research and development for Yamaha in the United States, he had to gauge in what directions the American motorcycle market might shift and what new Yamaha products could find buyers in the United States. So Hoel was curious: What was Dave Holeman doing?

Holeman was a desert racer. Head of Yamaha's technical publications in America, he was then going through his learn-by-falling-down stage in desert racing, and that learning process left any student with assorted bumps, scabs, and abrasions. Some of his fellow employees thought Holeman should report to work on Monday mornings with no more to show for the experience than a weight of silver sand in his lungs. That notion pictured the desert was some vast expanse of billowing white sand dunes, a harmless place to frolic.

The high desert in Southern California hardly resembled those visionary rolling dunes. The desert's elevations ranged from 130 feet below sea level at Death Valley to 6,500 feet in the high pine-tree forests. The popular play areas lay at about 3,000 feet. In places, the desert surface was sandy and rolling; in other areas the sharp rocks and hard soil could be as treacherous as a generous covering of broken bottles strewn over a concrete floor. The description even failed to do the surface full justice, because the floor itself could be cracked or wavy; varieties of cacti poked from the surface, and puckerbushes or cholla would swat the inattentive novice on the legs, or bring him to the ground full of needles. Hitting a break in the surface or walloping a fair-sized rock could likewise dislodge the motorcycle from the rider, whose hands locked on the handgrips with a vise-like clench. Taking a fall on the desert floor could produce a tumbling mass traveling at 60 mph and composed of equal parts motorcycle, sand, rocks, rider, and puckerbush. That was the reality of desert racing, and that is what Hoel went off to see one weekend in company with Holeman.

The desert was the best place to ride off-the-road in Southern California, because the desert was really off-road, off the beaten and unbeaten track, in 1966. In all the United States, there were very few motorcycle enthusiasts who actually rode motorcycles cross-country; most street riders regarded off-road riding as exotic and bizarre. All the practitioners of off-road sport might have filled a large closet, though one never knew for sure, because off-road riding was a hidden sport, undiscovered by government sociologists. Easterners disappeared into wooded hills and valleys, and in the West the desert swallowed large events whole. Traditionally, Americans had not thought much of the desert, having found attractive names for places there, such as Death Valley, and concluding that the desert was fit real estate for Air Force gunnery and for exploding a few experimental atomic bombs. In the minds of most Americans, deserts simply occupied space and not much more. Consequently, running motorcycles across the desert outraged no one.

At the appointed hour and place in the desert, Hoel saw two lines of motorcycles, large machines in the front row and smaller ones to the rear, all waiting dead-engined for the start. At the drop of the organizing club's banner, the riders lighted their engines and raced off toward a distant smoke bomb, where markers began defining the course across the high desert. The first wave, with the crisp barks of big, unmuffled, four-stroke engines shattering the desert serenity, left a few minutes ahead of the second wave of smaller, slower machines. No one ran a standard street machine cross-country on the desert; only highly modified street motorcycles could endure the hammering which high-speed desert racing inflicted upon machines. The pint-sized 90-cc and 100-cc motorcycles had been stripped and modified until only the frames and engines were still recognizable in the best examples. Big desert sleds invariably started life as 650-cc Triumph street machines; long hours of work would transform the motorcycle into a desert racer—a stark machine barren and devoid of all extraneous items, with a modified and strengthened running gear. By the time Hoel made his first desert sojourn with Holeman, however, the 650-cc desert sleds were going out of date.

The most impressive machines in the desert were 250-cc, two-stroke competition scramblers which gave the larger motorcycles fits. Products of British and European manufacturers, built especially for British-style scrambles and European-type motocross, these machines were—compared to the desert sleds—extraordinarily light and agile and maneuverable. They skimmed over the desert surface through which the big sleds cut. The performance of these machines—Greeves, Bultaco, Montesa, and Husqvarna—impressed Hoel, who might have dismissed any further thoughts about such motorcycles had it not been for two facts. First: Lightweight, single-cylinder, two-stroke motorcycles owned the future in dirt riding and all off-road competition. Second: Yamaha, as a major manufacturer of two-stroke motorcycles, could produce something along the lines of the two-stroke racing motorcycles which Hoel found in the desert. The appeal, Hoel reasoned, would have to be broader than just a two-stroke racer tailored for the Southern California high desert. So Hoel and Holeman wondered aloud whether or not Yamaha should try building a motorcycle which could be ridden on the street, and then, if the owner wished, entered in an off-road enduro with a minimum of preparation, or perhaps in a desert race with a bit more work. Such a motorcycle would have to be designed and developed for off-road use, but capable of street service.

This idea proceeded in a direction opposite to the normal state of things. Some manufacturers, including Yamaha, offered "street scramblers" or "scramblers" in their model line-ups, but these motorcycles were nothing more than transparent street bikes with high exhaust pipes and plates to guard the undersides of engines. If the owner wanted to make the motorcycle ready for real off-road duty, he had to hack and modify in order to build a serviceable off-road machine. On the other hand, genuine competition machines, such as the Greeves, could not be adapted to street use. Greeves could have made, without undue effort, a dual-purpose machine blending street and off-road characteristics. But Greeves didn't. As its main business, the company was busy turning out wheelchairs under government contract in England. Hoel and Holeman thought they knew what sort of motorcycle Yamaha should try to build, but they didn't quite know what to call it—maybe a dual-purpose bike, bred off the road instead of on the street.

The nearest thing to this concept which Holeman had ever seen was a Spanish motorcycle, the Montesa Scorpion, which had been brought into the United States in minute numbers two years earlier. Plagued by seizure problems and gearbox difficulties, the Montesa fell quickly to the sidelines. Yet, in idealized form, the Montesa had the idea; in 1964 it had simply been ahead of its time. At this point, Mike Sekine, project engineer for Yamaha International (the United States distributor), and Ike Kono, chief engineer, became involved in the Hoel-Holeman scheme. Kono and Sekine, both native Japanese on assignment in America from Yamaha in Japan, carefully weighed Hoel's idea. Thus began a liaison between Southern California and Japan which would produce the Yamaha DT-1, the most significant motorcycle to land in America

Below: In autumn, riders still roam the Pennsylvania hills. Far left: A good off-road machine, like the automatic-transmission Rokon, must motorboat as well as motorcycle. Near left: Montesa's trials bike is more at home picking through obstacle courses than buzzing open fields.

since the first Hondas. The DT-1 triggered an explosion of off-road motorcycles.

The Yamaha DT-1 was a prime example of a Japanese motorcycle created by remote control in the United States. Hoel went to Japan for a product-planning session, met with the Yamaha company's executives, with whom final decisions and responsibilities rested, and showed them 8-mm motion pictures of desert races. The movies flatly amazed the Japanese executives. They had never seen the desert before, nor a desert sled, nor such motorcycle competition. Hoel presented his case for the dual-purpose motorcycle, and he proved convincing. Hoel, almost visionary, was betting on his idea, and the Japanese decided to bet on him. Soon thereafter, through Hoel's doorway in Southern California, passed a collection of sample motorcycles destined for Japan: Greeves, Montesa, Husqvarna, Bultaco, among others. Then in the last half of 1966, the prototype Yamaha machine arrived. Warehouse workmen at Yamaha International in California had taken a peek inside the shipping crate, and those who saw the thing didn't know what it was, or even what it was supposed to be. Hoel, Holeman, and Sekine swooped up the bike and carted it off to a small, abandoned room in the warehouse area. It was tagged the 007 Room, and the prototype was kept there under lock and key.

The motorcycle was a composite of ideas drawn from Hoel, Holeman, the sample motorcycles, and the Yamaha engineering department. The green motorcycle had a one-off, hand-welded frame which seemed to have more weld by weight than frame tubing. A frumpy tank and abbreviated saddle rested on top of the machine, and the bike carried full lighting and electrical equipment. Forks, shock absorbers, and wheels made up the suspension system. The engine was a 250-cc, single-cylinder, two-stroke unit with oil injection and a five-speed gearbox.

The work began in earnest. Hoel, Holeman, Sekine, and Kono would take the motorcycle out into the desert, try it, change and modify parts, take photographs. Test session by test session, they kept Japan updated by photographs, airmail reports, and Telex communiqués. The engine gave no problems, nor had any been expected —though a 250-cc, single-cylinder engine was huge for the period. Laboratory experimentation in Japan could perfect the engine. The hard part—the desert—was in Southern California. The mysteries involved matching the chassis and running gear to the American off-road environment and, specifically, to the high desert. The Yamaha development clique had one basic operating assumption: If the motorcycle would withstand the desert environment and behave well over that forsaken terrain, the bike would work well in almost any kind of off-road riding area which could be found in the United States.

The clique needed the experience and expertise of a chassis and suspension genius, so Holeman invited Neil Fergus to the test sessions; Fergus had captured the Number One plate in desert racing on a four-stroke Honda twin; the machine had been so drastically modified that it was more a Fergus than a Honda. The favorite test area in the desert included three in-series whoop-dee-doos, thus named for the messages which the rider's stomach-pit sent to his mouth whenever such a section was taken at speed. The roller-coaster strip had three crests separated by two dips. If a machine's frame and suspension were lacking, the rider would know it by the time he reached the third rise—because the motorcycle's handlebars would be a blur, slapping lock-to-lock, and the motorcycle would pitch sideways when it went airborne off the third rise. There followed a dull thud inside a cloud of dust.

The prototype, which at first did a number of foul landings, was eventually coaxed toward more civil behavior by all kinds of changes: different swinging arms, shock absorbers, springs, fork clamps, and more. The changes were duly recorded and sent back to Japan. Visiting engineers, over from Japan, stood dumbfounded at the high desert—and the testing going on there. Even though the environment was totally alien, back in Japan the engineers were creating a motorcycle for off-road service in the desert and elsewhere. The difficulty of the task was enormous: The engineers were designing a new kind of motorcycle for a place totally outside their experience. By comparison, building a street machine seemed easy; everyone knew what an asphalt road was like. While Japan stayed abreast of developments in the desert by Telex, the prototype machine itself remained the final statement of the development work. At last, late in 1966, the five-man clique on the American side—Hoel, Holeman, Fergus, Sekine, and Kono—crated up the much modified and changed prototype and sent it back to Japan, confident that it had been sufficiently developed in three months of off-road desert testing. The prototype, they thought, once back in Japan, could serve as the pattern for future Yamaha production models.

Two days later there arrived in California two preproduction models from Japan. The Yamaha factory team had moved so quickly that it had not waited for the prototype to return to the factory. The engineering department virtually had designed the production model from the reports sent back from the United States. That meant the prototype, which held the final bits of critical information, would arrive too late to have any determining influence on the first production models—or any others for the next five years. With a certain sense of foreboding, Hoel, Fergus, and Holeman took one new preproduction model out to the whoop-dee-doo testing ground. The suspension units still weren't right, and most of all, the frame held the engine too high and the steering was a bit too quick. The motorcycle pitched sideways over the third rise, and landed with a thud in a puff of dust. Hoel and

Holeman were disappointed. Fergus was sick. While the motorcycle was acceptable—and far better than the undeveloped prototype—the preproduction version did not handle not nearly as well as the developed prototype. The development clique had wanted something near perfect; in their view, the motorcycle was satisfactory. The production mapping in Japan was too far advanced to change the motorcycle in any significant way. Holeman ventured that the bike would sell, Hoel nodded his agreement. They left their desert test site. And so Yamaha introduced their DT-1, and waited. Not for long.

Dealers deluged Yamaha International with orders for the new dual-purpose motorcycle, a reflection of the enthusiasm dealers found for the machine among their customers. The development clique thought the DT-1 was a "right" motorcycle because the concept behind the bike was solid. The response almost flabbergasted the developers. Common sense suggested that a dual-purpose machine, developed off the road instead of on the pavement, could have a following. But no one at Yamaha was quite prepared for the cheering reception. The Yamaha DT-1 had caught the Great Outdoor Revival in America in its waking hour.

There was something of a religion about the Great Outdoors in the late sixties. Like Technology before it, the Great Outdoors flowered into a Pop deity. It was worth wondering how much substance there was in this religion; ritual and symbolic acts seemed to satisfy its requirements. People who never would hike bought hiking boots; a lot of camping gear went on one or two outings and then into permanent storage; trailers and camping vehicles first took owners on vacation and then made the neighborhood rental circuit. Americans bought things which had all the important code words of the late 1960's etched into them: freedom, liberation, escape, purity, honesty, fun, reality. Most people could not flee from other

*North America provides widely
different settings for off-road
riding. Building a
"go-anywhere" vehicle is
tough, especially when the "anywhere"
might be New York snow, or
heat and dust in an overland race
in Baja California,
or an oceanfront in Florida.*

people. They could only make symbolic gestures in consumptive desperation.

The Yamaha DT-1 had "off-road America" stamped all over it. The motorcycle certainly didn't fit the Japanese idea of a machine for the road. As a street motorcycle, the DT-1 had been seriously compromised by its design and development for dirt riding. The design concept, which required a lightweight, agile motorcycle, worked against the DT-1 on the street. For example, no Japanese manufacturer would have considered making a distilled street machine with a 250-cc, single-cylinder, two-stroke engine. That kind of engine design was inherently too rough-running for pleasant, civilized riding on the road. Most riders, the Japanese thought, would not accept a vibrating street motorcycle, nor would they care to do without the convenience of electric starting. An electric starter was out of the question for an off-road motorcycle; the weight penalty was much too high. Such things as engine vibration and kickstarting were only the beginning of the DT-1's design trade-offs against street riding; the motorcycle simply lacked proper Japanese sophistication and civility for road use.

The Yamaha DT-1 was a simple, basic machine. For the same reason that few people would consider an open-air, four-wheel-drive military vehicle a very satisfactory passenger car, Yamaha engineers and executives —and the development clique itself—would have hardly expected that the DT-1, and its successors and imitators, would appeal to motorcyclists who would not be trailing off into the wilderness, or even into a nearby pasture. The situation confounded. Enthusiasts bought off-road machines like the DT-1, but they never really used them for their designed and developed purpose. It was enough to drive a good businessman into a bewildering, closing circle. Dual-purpose machines, with off-road printed all over them, were cheerfully purchased and ridden almost exclusively on the street. The conclusion was nearly irresistible: Buying an off-road motorcycle in the DT-1 pattern was a way to celebrate the Great Outdoors without really trucking much with it.

Trail riding for pleasure seemed such a reasonable proposition inside the United States. Why should dual-purpose motorcycles hide out on the streets? There were still wide-open spaces in the United States. In a space-intensive country, widespread pleasure riding off the public roads would have been largely unthinkable. In Europe, off-road riding had to be organized into controlled events in which a maximum number of riders used a minimum amount of space. That restrictive concept was both out of touch with all the American code words of Great Outdoors, and out of place in a space-extensive country. But if the United States had space, there was not nearly so much for pleasure trail riding as casual observers might at first have thought.

An enthusiast could dabble in the Great Outdoors with an off-road machine like Yamaha's DT-1. Although only a minority of dabblers ever turned into confirmed trail riders, the absolute number of off-road motorcyclists did jump in the late 1960's and early 1970's. In some parts of the country, notably Southern California, motorcyclists had to hunt longer and harder to find private or public land for pleasure trail riding. American off-road riders got caught in a vise: Increasing numbers of off-road enthusiasts rode in a seemingly decreasing amount of space. Motorcyclists were only minor participants in the political taffy pull on the Great Outdoors. Competing factions—recreational vehicles, industry, conservation elements, bureaucracies—were tugging away at different angles. Almost every interest donned Great Outdoors face-masks and swore allegiance to conservation. On a practical level, the result for motorcycling was fairly simple. Those enthusiasts with quenchless interest in riding motorcycles

off-road could still locate areas; with more difficulty, the novice trial rider—only casually interested in the sport—could test his real attachment.

Off-road motorcycling is a far more demanding sport than street riding. The first demand is a physical one, because off-road terrain is sufficiently rough in most places to mete out varying degrees of physical punishment. Unless the trail rider has stayed in reasonably good physical shape, or still is under twenty-five years of age, body aches and pains will reward his trail-riding effort. Though a sport for the young, age alone will not protect one from the distresses which accompany the hardening process of trail riding. Those unaccustomed to day-long rides may greet the evening by limping toward the medicine chest, searching for liniment and aspirin.

Highways cross streams and vault over rivers on bridges; trails meet obstacles directly. Highway engineers spend lifetimes leveling out grades, bypassing difficult passes, and smoothing down surfaces. Off-road trails ignore most monuments to civil engineering. Even gentle logging roads fall victim to mud, ruts, and quick little streams. No matter how slowly it is taken, a good day of off-road riding will strain beginners.

Beyond physical grit, off-road motoring demands a certain mechanical competence from the rider. On the street, should the motorcycle stop, the motorcyclist, if baffled into capitulation, can stash the motorcycle or ring for road service. On the trail, if something goes awry, the alternatives are clear: Fix it or walk out.

A confirmed off-road rider can be no dabbler. He must seek out new riding areas, enjoy the physical exertion, and have the skill to service his motorcycle. The road conditions which Cannonball Baker described on his 1914 transcontinental dash could be drawn out of the modern off-road rider's logbook. In a very fundamental way, off-road riding is primitive motorcycling.

Those simple, stark, off-road motorcycles charm a great number of enthusiasts who like the functional, economical appearance of the machines. The motorcycles carry little gratuitous baggage. Function rather than civility rules their design and development. Function nets spare, serviceable motorcycles and frill-less mechanical objects. For example, lighting systems—compared to those of street motorcycles—can be quickly detached and shelved. Single-cylinder, two-stroke engines are simple, straightforward. Covers, mufflers, and panels don't interfere with quick servicing. Off-road machines can be disassembled and reassembled swiftly, and that quality is important to lovers of nuts and bolts. Off-road machines retain that basic first quality of classic machines: Lever A pivots on fulcrum B and moves rod C.

Enthusiasts who put space, time, and machinery together in trail riding find pleasures seldom reached in street riding. The communication between rider and machine is amplified in off-road riding. For most enthusiasts, a street machine telegraphs back to the rider at a low output, and the better the machine's running gear, the less intrusive the motorcycle's telegraphy may be. A low-level thrum might characterize its behavior. Smooth road surfaces help to moderate suspension activity, while fast, bumpy corners boost the inputs the rider receives from the machine. Clearly, as most street machines approach their limits on cornering, the thrum develops some excited blips which the rider's mind and body immediately pick up: A rear tire slips out in a series of little skips, or the handlebars begin to move against hands and wrists in a gentle wag. The machine feels as though it comes alive because it develops movements which operate in directions separate from the main track of motion through the corner. This does not mean that a street machine says nothing to a rider until the edge of adhesion is reached and disaster begins. The impulses which proceed from the road through the machine and into the enthusiast's body just remain modulated. The thrum is always there.

Riding off the road heightens the rider's awareness of the machine's activity, because the motorcycle communicates at an amplified level all the time. Rough terrain produces gross reactions in motorcycles; the footing of the bike is neither as firm nor as constant as on pavement. The off-road motorcycle may spend a great deal of time in the air. The machine always feels very much alive; there's a lot of motion outside the tracking course of the vehicle. All this motion demands an active participation on the part of the rider, who must read the upcoming topography, meet it, respond with the bike to the terrain, and deal with the bike's reaction to the terrain. This involvement with the terrain and the machine—with riding—is more intense and complete than most motorcycle riders experience on a street machine. The participation is so consuming that 30 mph on the dirt can make 90 mph on the highway fade into dullness. The sheer activity and exhilaration of off-road riding makes low-numbered speeds insignificant. Though off-road riding has its hazards—puckerbush needles and hard rocks and trees—human beings can endure 20-mph bounce-offs in the dirt much easier than 70-mph get-offs on pavement. The enthusiast can learn at his own pace, matching speed and terrain to his level of skill. The dirt rider senses the progress he makes in dirt riding; he can measure improvement in new obstacles cleared, sand washes negotiated, new hills climbed, and mudholes conquered.

At some point, a rider's expertise and speed may create a kind of stimulus overload from the machine, which will dance in frenzy under him. At this ultralevel, the differences between good-handling machines and bad ones actually diminish, as good handlers and bad are forced to operate in a range far beyond their suspension limits. The rider loses consciousness of the machine as the intervening medium between the surface and his mind. It is almost a case of mind working directly on matter. Transcendental motorcycling, always difficult to touch, can better be reached on rough terrain than at terrific speeds over asphalt roads.

Not all pleasures of off-road riding are so rarefied. Riding off the paved highways brings a tremendous sense of freedom and emancipation. A rider can make his own speed; he has no cars crowding up behind him or long impassable strings of cars out front. The off-road rider need not hum along great concrete and asphalt channels, bounded by prescriptive signs, on-and-off ramps, and the unending sounds and smells and dangers of competing traffic. An empty, silent trail on a peaceful day, secluded from a hectic week, has a tranquility that only sticks to brief hours. That freedom comes with finding a place where the environment is clear of the handiworks of man, and where the enthusiast can shape a day away from the interfering hands of others. With a machine to serve his changing moods, he can rush toward a distant mountain on a wide-open plain, or troll along a time-forgotten trail with only a whispering exhaust for company.

That kind of freedom, however fleeting, is a solitary thing, for the enthusiast is alone inside his own helmet. Comradeship there is on the trail, and good friends to share the day. But off-road motorcycles are monoposto machines—a passenger would just disrupt the communication between man and machine. Single seats are only fitting, as the trail-riding experience is a private thing, though done in groups. It illustrates that old axiom: When two do the same thing, it's not the same thing after all.

In the most severe test of off-road riding talent, many must do the same thing, and in strict team co-ordination. The International Six Days' Trial is a test which goes on for six days, with international teams of motorcyclists riding over a prescribed course on a prescribed schedule;

Off-road overland competition came of age in America when the United States played host to the International Six Days' Trial in 1973. The event, strung out over long daily cross-country loops, runs on an intricate scoring system. Spectators, wanting to see the world's best collection of off-road riders, hiked into the Berkshire Mountains in Massachusetts for close-up investigations.

falling off schedule nets scoring penalties against individual competitors and their national teams. The cross-country courses used for ISDT events, linking good and bad dirt roads with overland trails, would reduce most pleasure trail riders to hikers in short order. So would the distances. Some days, the teamsters must ride over 200 miles. The ISDT competitors rank among the best off-road riders in the world, and the best mechanics, too, since the riders must deal with any emergency machine problems by soldiering through and setting things right—or at least operational—again. In most cases the cure must come out of the rider's tool pouch and his head.

The central prize is the World Team Championship Trophy, which is awarded for the best performance by a national team of six riders; the six motorcycles in the team must include at least two different displacement classes. So fierce is the competition that two or three brilliant riders cannot make up for three or four lackluster performers. Great success depends upon the absence or minimum of error by all six riders. While other awards have changed and grown, and while the rules have been adjusted to meet new competitive realities, the ISDT's essential character has stayed constant: It's a friendly war between national states. Though the greatest prestige attaches to the World Trophy, an array of other prizes exists: the International Silver Vase, the Watling Trophy, the Club Team Diploma, the Manufacturer's Team Award. And finally FIM medals—bronze, silver, and gold—recognize individual achievements within a team framework.

The ISDT is an intricate game in which individual efforts must be painstakingly orchestrated to over-all team purposes. Given the complicated scoring system and the high stakes of national honor, the ISDT is a cross between computer chess and mechanized warfare. Chiseling, less tolerated in individual sports, has been refined into sophisticated fifth-column mechanical help. Since the ISDT is supposed to be a test of reliability, only riders should work on the machines—and the motorcycles should not be replaced piece by piece over the six days. To this end, all major components of each motorcycle are marked before the competition begins, and all motorcycles are impounded every evening. But time and places exist for clandestine repairs during any day of competition. An isolated nook in a remote woods might teem with hidden mechanics.

A rider, for example, might start a day's ride with a seriously dented wheel rim and make a predetermined, secret rendezvous with team mechanics who replace the entire wheel assembly. Later in the day, the mechanics meet the rider at another secret point and quick-change wheel assemblies again, so that the rider finishes the day with the original hub—a marked part—and a new round rim. In most cases, individual riders cope with their own problems without outside team assistance, but most national teams are prepared to replace the irreparable if they must. The national teams in ISDT excel in slyness and fast mechanical slight of hand.

International trials have long been a peculiarly European form of motorcycle sport. American enthusiasts had traditionally held enduros, events run cross-country on marked routes at predetermined speed averages, but the contests in the United States were not tied to nationalism. Yankee events had—and still have—individual winners. Europeans fell into international competition naturally. Many of the countries crowded together on part of the Continent had motorcycle industries. And, being close rivals, they were also warm rivals.

Riders also were far better organized in Europe than in America. They did their off-road riding in groups. Independent trail riding was an unknown concept. Clubs rode against one another, and so it followed that nations should, too. Europeans stressed club and country.

The United States had no continental rivals;

Americans owned a large piece of real estate in the Western Hemisphere, and 3,000 miles of water divorced the Yankees from European sport. Distance didn't mean complete isolation, since reliability trials, not much different from contemporary British events, were part of the American scene until they withered away in the 1920's. The American sport eventually got off the road, but never in the thoroughly organized way the Europeans managed. In the first place, enthusiasts could find space to go trail riding for pleasure if they so desired. Second, American competitive events emphasized individual winners.

Sectional rivalry there was in the United States. Combative feelings between off-road enduro riders, East and West, had the scent of European-style political motoring. The rivalry had its roots in the differences between eastern terrain and that of the West, especially Southern California's. Michigan's Jack Pine Enduro represented the best eastern version of the sport, while the Greenhorn Enduro offered the toughest western model. With one exception, no western enduro rider ever won the Michigan event, and the Greenhorn refused to yield victory to any eastern rider. In the East, parts of enduros were run on roads—secondary trails through wood and valley, with lots of mud and water along the way. Out West, large sections of desert wilderness, unchartered by trails, provided running ground for enduros. Riders who could master the desert conditions couldn't match eastern riders in the mud. And conversely, those riders who grew up competing east of the Mississippi River couldn't defeat the western enduro riders in the desert.

So vastly different were the environments that the rules which worked in the East were inadequate when applied to the western landscape. In eastern enduros, for example, written directions and occasional markers were sufficient to guide riders along routes which were fairly well defined. But in the West, there were not always trails in the accepted eastern sense; in the trackless desert, enduros ran on sight-to-sight markers. There was no other way. Indeed, Southern Californians had to write a regional supplement to the national rulebook produced by the American Motorcycle Association in Ohio. If there were regional variations in the rules, motorcycles used in enduros likewise showed differences East to West. Western riders considered eastern motorcycles much too fragile to be trusted in the desert. Western conditions had a reputation for mauling eastern-developed machines—unless they had been strengthened. And in the East, western bikes were considered overweight and musclebound.

The East-West controversy extended to American participation in the International Six Days' Trial in 1973. Should the Americans host the event in Fort Hood, Texas, where western riding conditions prevailed? Or should the ISDT be held in the East on ground more familiar to Europeans? First Fort Hood became the site. Westerners were enthusiastic; the world would see how well Europeans would fare in America's special regional playground. Then the AMA, reckoning its advantage, reversed itself and changed the site to New England. Any American edge disappeared.

At the forty-eighth International Six Days' Trial, held in 1973 in the Berkshire Mountains of Massachusetts, American spectators, many of whom were only casual weekend trail riders, stood in awe at the riding and mechanical skills of the international riders. It was the first time that most American enthusiasts had seen such riders, because it was the first time the ISDT had ever been held in the United States. The Czechoslovakian team won the World Trophy again. Anyone in Dalton, Massachusetts, during ISDT week in 1973 could hear a dozen foreign tongues—in hotel lobbies, in restaurants, on the course, in the impound area—and know that the motorcycle world had grown both larger and smaller. And all for the better.

19.

MOTOCROSS

Motocross is so American that it's a wonder Americans didn't invent it. That thought jiggled around in my mind as I stood clapping my hands in Elkhorn, Wisconsin, one chill day in late 1970. The clapping had nothing to do with the motocross activity of the moment and everything to do with warding off the cold which came sneaking through my gloves. In truth, the day couldn't have been a real Wisconsin bone-freezer, since the heavy skies from time to time released a finely strained rain that left a glassy sheen on everything it dampened. Thousands of spectators mustered out that day to see European motocross stars, to see how genuine motocross professionals dealt with mud, hills, ruts, jumps, bogs, and wetness on the closed circuit, lap after lap. The best Americans were taking their laps, too, as well as invited locals; but the natives were obliging home-grown fodder for the European cannon. Everyone loved the show, because it was such a show.

The motocross spectators, damp though they were and reasonable candidates for pneumonia, had much to seize their attention. You could press up against the snow fence and literally touch riders and machines as they went past, lurching, bounding, and flying. The viewing distance stayed close-range. Distance never bleached color and intensity out of the racing. Close up, the spectator didn't have to imagine what the motorcycle might be doing. He could see the suspension working, rider errors large and small, the quick corrections and little saves, faces blank with concentration and bodies limp with fatigue, and bright jerseys gone dull under coatings of mud. The spectators could watch the motocrossers run through the woods, with the fastest motorcycles speeding in long skips, touching down—it seemed—just to gain a sense of direction, then leaping ahead with such fury that the ground almost seemed to kick them off of its surface. The lightweight two-stroke racing bikes lapped the course with churlish rasps trailing from the expansion chambers.

After ten laps of a heat, the leaders had already caught up with the also-rans, and viewers had to know individual riders in order to keep tabs on the race. To the untutored eye, the event could have all the confusion of a fifty-member cat-and-dog fight. Except for one saving grace. The fast riders danced over the course so much faster than the great body of entrants that the speed and grace of the superexperts easily tagged them as the leaders.

Both leaders and runners could be engaged in bike-to-bike combat, with the machines leapfrogging madly, touching at times but never quite colliding. And back in the pack, jumbles of competitors, traveling in knots, struggled with one another and the course. Off-road riders in the gallery can appreciate the riding more fully than others, but even casual observers see enough to leave their mouths agape. Motocross has everything: color, noise, close-up action, compactness, accessibility, local adaptability.

To say that motocross was actually invented suggests a more conscious effort than the past records. Motocross just grew. Its history remains locked in a thousand individual minds. Unlike road racing, born in the flash and heat of publicity, motocross just happened along haphazardly and piecemeal, almost defying documentation. From the beginning, road racing enjoyed manufacturers' support, which invested the sport with importance. The road-racing setting on the Continent and on the Isle of Man reeked with significance—whereupon journalists so testified in page and print. By comparison, motocross origins were amateur and populist.

It probably all began with two enthusiasts, long since forgotten, who raced across virgin country on a bet. The first organized event on record, though it was not called motocross, was a race held on Camberley Heath, England, in February, 1924. The local clubmen, it seemed, wanted to stage their own southern version of the timed and

Opening pages: It looks
like war, but it's really motocross
weekend/American-style.
Helmets, goggles, mouth and chest
protectors arm riders against
the terrain and fellow competitors.
Below: Less protected but
equally determined are riders
competing in the British Grand Prix.

Motocrossers do not roll over terrain. Motocrossing involves flying a motorcycle across roughery in a series of leaps, hops, and bounds. Opposite: Bryan Wade, the great Greeves hope, hurries the 380-cc two-stroke along. Below: Andy Roberton flies a 350 BSA banger. Bottom: Bengt Aberg powers his Husqvarna uphill.

observed Scott Trial, run annually in Yorkshire. There was to be a difference however. Southerners wanted to scrub the observed sections, wherein motorcyclists cleared difficult obstacles under the scrutiny of judges who penalized clumsy performances. But that change would turn the Southern Scott Trial into a speed contest alone. The Auto-Cycle Union, the national governing body of the motorcycle sport in England was horrified at the proposal, and withheld its sanction on the grounds that the Southern Scott Trial couldn't possibly be a timed and observed trial *without* the observed sections. Not to be put off so easily, the southerners searched for an indigenous title, ultimately settling on the "Southern Scott Scramble." The scramble was run over two laps, with a suitable lunch interval in between laps.

English-style scrambles, as time passed, captured a following of amateurs who regarded dirt racing as low-pressure, low-budget fun. Machinery preparation required little more effort than removing headlamps, taillights, and mufflers—and, for the affluent, the fitting of knobby tires. In the early days, scramble courses were laid out in rudimentary fashion, the object being to ride from Point A to Point B, and then back to Point A in the fastest time, and by the most convenient route. Inevitably, properly closed circuits added to spectator appeal, as it was important for the onlookers to know where the course was, if for no other reason than to avoid being hit when stepping out from behind a tree. Twin rows of flags marked out the enclosed course. If the progress toward controlled, comprehensible events pleased most observers, the purists were heard to snort "sissy bloody path racers." According to the purists, *real* scrambles included bottomless bogs, impossible hills, big boulders, and deep sand. Anything less was blasphemy.

In the days before World War II, demonstrating the reliability of basically standard street bikes was the purists' central aim, and that was just as well, for standard motorcycles were all the British or continental amateur had to run. Motorcycles were a socially and economically acceptable—though not always admired—means of transportation. For some, they were the only form of personal motorized transport possible. So it was no accident that scrambling, as well as other forms of motor sport in England and Europe, had a strong "reliability" emphasis. Private owners could hardly think of their machines as consumable, disposable items. Motorcycles were supposed to be reliable; if they couldn't manage that, they weren't much good for transportation or sport. One basic machine —which served weekly transport needs—could be stripped for scrambles, long-distance reliability trials, grass-track racing, hill climbs, and other sorts of competition. If an amateur could conquer a hill on a street-legal 1,000-cc V-twin that carried all its road equipment, then he was really some motorcyclist.

Scrambling was so amateur, and the market so small, that it discouraged manufacturers from spending the effort and resources to build specialized scrambles machines. Factory-built scrambles motorcycles only deviated from basic street machines in minor respects, thereby upsetting production schedules as little as possible. Scramblers were stripped-at-the-factory models—which was very much in keeping with the amateur sport, for that was exactly the way the competitors made *their* scramblers! All the factories did was to save the purchasers some effort.

The French turned British scrambling into motocross after World War II. Across the Channel the continentals contrived a distinct form, separate from that raging in England. That seemed only fair, since British scrambling began as a sporting deviant anyway. Stories filtered back to England concerning the exciting new French *moto-cross,* and how it was transforming scrambles.

No one knew whether *moto-cross* merely meant French scrambles, or if the multiheat scoring system, now so familiar to motocross calculations, had been employed from the beginning. Apparently, motocross originated as straight-race scrambling, but somewhere along the line in France the concept of finding an over-all winner from two or three races (heats or legs) took hold.

If the timing of the transition is uncertain, the reasons for the French scoring system are clear. In Great Britain, the scramble calendar consisted of dozens of national and local meetings, and with entry lists containing a vast number of riders. Fields of 300 motorcyclists passed as unremarkable. Obviously, many races had to be run in order to provide outings for all the competitors, and there was nothing unusual about having twenty winners going home at the end of a day's sport. In contrast, French motocross was sport for professionals, all of whom demanded payment upon appearance. French spectators insisted upon seeing paid performers. As a matter of economics, French promoters restricted the professional contingent to ten or fifteen riders, and then swelled out the field with local (and unpaid) heroes. With only a small number of contestants to handle, three lengthy races could feature identical line-ups, sometimes keeping the ultimate winner's identity in doubt to the very end. There weren't enough local amateurs to make up a day-long

racing program of the sort found in England—even if French crowds could have been persuaded to forsake professionals. So the French, logically, ran the same riders three times. The French system made sure the paid performers earned their keep, gave the spectators their francs' worth of racing, and made a profit besides.

France gave motocross real impetus when, in the late 1940's and early 1950's, they discovered that staging a motocross race was easier and more profitable than a road-racing promotion. With great Gallic imagination, holes in the ground were transformed into motocross spectaculars with the courses looping up and down the vertical sides of hills and cliffs. From the outset, French organizers extended themselves to involve the local dignitaries and populace, including the famed, almost mandatory, open-pipe parades through town squares. The French, and other continentals, staged motocross events with the same openness they had toward road races. If a section of public road had to be shut down to hold the event, then the roadway was indeed sealed off. In France and Belgium particularly, no large social purpose was served by hiding motocross racing out of sight and sound. In England, the organizers were happy to accommodate the local townspeople and closet the event if necessary. The French promoters, busy developing a professional event *à la française*, weren't happy until the local populace

The Belgians, indeed most continentals, bring a sense of participation to a motocross race. That feeling transforms certain events into institutions which need not be hidden at the outskirts of town. At the Circuit de Citadele, Namur, Belgium, motocross is a center-stage event.

almost became participants in the motocross event.

At Namur in Belgium, for example, the stage is set in a public, open space of the historic Citadel which towers alongside the town. From the arena, where there are cafe and bar facilities, *course-Namur* snakes perilously close to local habitats before plunging through a forest, where trees line the circuit and sprout in the middle of the track. At one point, the motocross takes to a public, paved road which skirts a pub, thus allowing a lucky few to watch the action and drink beer at the same time, a favorite Belgian pastime which surpasses motocross and soccer. Those spectators who have not put themselves under roof cheerfully endure their North Sea climate of variable and unpredictable weather. Belgians enjoy themselves at motocross, and the crowds are nothing if not partisan. They have been known to lengthen corners for foreign riders and form instant shortcuts for local heroes. Nor will they brook poor performances by riders. Flying clods of earth and empty beer cans indicate spectator disgust at poor rider effort. This shouldn't suggest that Belgians are *the* European motocross spectators, since enthusiasm spreads far and wide. Italy, Spain, Austria, Germany, Czechoslovakia, Sweden, the Netherlands—every country is grabbed by some aspect of motocross. The sport has all the ingredients for universal appeal.

When the Fédération Internationale Motorcycliste (FIM) created the European and World Championships, motocross scoring fell easily and logically into the scheme of things, with the French system being adopted. In the early postwar period, many of the machines originated in Great Britain. Nor were the motorcycles highly specialized machines. In the 1947 *Moto-cross des Nations* at The Hague, the Netherlands, one Dutchman ran a Triumph twin, complete with low-slung exhausts, big, bulbous fuel tank, rigid frame, and spring saddle. No wonder he retired after clobbering a tree.

Changes were on the way. In the late 1940's, the English, still engrossed in scrambling, used updates of pre-war designs fitted out with telescopic forks. Frames were rigid-rear-end models until swinging-arm rear suspension arrived. Before long, British factories enthusiastically embraced scrambling, and practically every known brand had pretentions to a factory team. For one thing, scrambling was a lot cheaper than road racing for most British factories. The big single-cylinder, four-stroke machines were still only lights-and-mufflers away from street thumpers. Factory interest in England also produced the first British scrambles-motocross professionals.

The new professionals were characters whose riding taxed equipment. Geoff Ward, for example, rose from novice to star rider in no time, and on an AJS he became a famous breaker of gearboxes. He was also adept

*Below: Bill Nilsson runs through
sticky going with an Eso 500 banger.
Right: René Baeter, the 1958
500-cc Champion, manhandles an FN
with telescopic forks;
earlier FN models had rubber-band front
suspension. Right bottom: When
Suzuki and Yamaha arrived to motocross
in Europe, two-strokes dominated.*

189

*Preceding pages: Sunday
afternoon traffic jams occur on
motocross tracks when youthful
American amateur racers channel
into the first corner after a
massed start. Right: Congestion and
frustration there may be—
and dreams of running open and free,
away from the oppressive crowd.*

at shearing off foot pegs like carrots when landing off big jumps. The new professionals also innovated. Les Archer won the 1956 500-cc World Championship in motocross with a single-overhead-camshaft Norton special. These Britons, and many more, campaigned regularly on the Continent, following the wheel tracks of the very early postwar trailblazers whose names and feats escaped all record books.

Motocross machinery began to change and become more specialized in the late 1950's. Up to Les Archer's 1956 Championship, modified street bikes, principally Belgian FN and Sarolea machines, dominated the 500-cc class of international motocross. Archer's Norton, which utilized Norton's overhead-camshaft racing engine retuned for motocross work, started a trend to specials, a movement which the Swedes adopted and expanded through 1963. Husqvarna, Monark, Lito, Crescent—the tank emblems announced the company of origin, but the motorcycles were a confusion of bits-and-pieces engines. The common ambition was to produce a lot of slogging power. Tractor-like, the machines would pull through gum and goo, or climb the steepest hill with the engine just barely beating out revolutions. Though remarkably tractable, the big 500's were also fast. Unleashed at hills with a straight third-gear approach, the bangers would blast uphill. Those factory mounts were 80-mph tractors.

The "Special Era" was the best ever for spectators. With the Swedish inventions, the British bangers, and the Czechoslovakian bikes, individual machines were identifiable and so were their noises. Protective coverall kits for the riders had not yet been developed, so spectators could pick out riders who did not look like escapees from gladiator rings. The heavy motorcycles might dive off a jump, touch down with metal crunches, and go into handling convulsions. Motocross riders had to be superfit to handle such antics. The very best riders could cope with bucking and weaving heavyweights which unceremoniously dumped off lesser talents.

The specials reached one kind of end point with the creation of the Swede Nils Hedlund. His big single-cylinder motorcycle had a bottom end which was basically Husqvarna. Upstairs, the engine carried a double-overhead-camshaft cylinder head of Hedlund's own design. The gearbox was BSA, the rear wheel Norton. Up front, the German Prenafa hub spun inside front forks which had Norton legs slotted into Ceriani yokes. The motorcycle was monstrously heavy, weighing in at 350 pounds. And its nose-heaviness compounded its obesity. This kind of heavy special was a result of the Swedish formula for success, which combined brute power with semiexotic engines, a concept that was nearly worn out. "Lightweight" was a relative and abused term. In 1962, Husqvarna, for example, could describe their heavyweight as "one of the finest and lightest motocross models ever built."

Meanwhile, in England the scrambling Rickman brothers—Don and Derek—turned away from the special-engine school of motocross development and focused their effort on weight and handling characteristics. Their philosophy proved so successful that quite ordinary engines, such as Triumph twins, became winners. The Rickmans' open secret was their Metisse frame and accessories, which lopped seventy pounds off the normal weight of 500-cc machines, put weight and strength in the right places, set new standards for craftsmanship, and raised handling qualities to a different league. In 1959 the Rickmans built a Triumph-powered, BSA-framed, Norton-forked mongrel which they dubbed Metisse. Two years later, they had abandoned the bits-and-pieces approach and produced a complete running gear. Still later, they marketed Metisse kits. By mid-1964, the small Rickman plant had shipped more than 500 frames to various domestic and European destinations, and a few landed in the United States. 1964

192

*Below: Vlastimili Valek leads
Jeff Smith. Valek's Jawa two-stroke was
all power and very little control;
Smith's BSA was the last hurrah
in lightweight four-strokes. Opposite
and bottom: Production racing
two-strokes for amateurs eventually
possessed power, handling,
reliability, and low-number weights.*

was *the* year of the Metisse. Some line-ups in 500-cc motorcross boasted a fifty percent Metisse strength. Even a significant number of Swedish motocrossers had become Metisse addicts.

Development of motocross equipment moved toward a balancing of low weight, reasonable power, outstanding handling, and reliability. This progression no longer made it possible to strip a street model, mount knobby tires, and have a go at British scrambling or European motocross. You needed a "special" of some sort. Then there came a time when even a special Rickman 500-cc motocross bike could get no smaller, because it had to house a 500 Triumph twin or a big Matchless single. Whereupon someone might have asked: Why not construct a "bigger" 250 motocross machine in order to get a smaller 500 motocrosser? That was a fair question, engaging enough to start the Rickmans building a "Petite-Metisse" powered by a 250-cc Spanish Bultaco engine. But by 1962 others had already anticipated such a movement.

If one raced 500-cc international motocross, it was difficult to take 250-cc motorcycles seriously. When the FIM put the 250's on the motocross calendar in 1957, they were considered devices to be suffered, and, if possible, banished to some obscure championship where they couldn't foul up *real* motocross. Four-stroke, single-cylinder bangers for the 500-cc World Championship, and the dreadful two-strokes for the 250-cc title—so thought contemporary riders—and never the paths should cross.

But cross they would. The seeds of two-stroke engine domination in the 500-cc class were sown by the British in the mid-1950's. In the first place, the capacity class lines in British scrambles became increasingly blurred with "Allcomers Races," which swept together machines from 150 cc to 500 cc. The Allcomers gave the upstart small bikes something to shoot at: bagging all the 500's and an over-all win. Into this Allcomers confusion walked a nonconformist—Bert Greeves—who evidently became a motorcycle manufacturer as a way of occupying his spare time.

Greeves concentrated on competition models because he was convinced that everyone else was doing things all wrong. They had spring suspension and hydraulic damping; Greeves had rubber-in-torsion springing and mechanical dampers. They had tubular frames; Greeves had a conglomeration of castings, tubes, and flat plates. And they stopped laughing when the Greeves' started to skip over the roughery at an alarming rate. But those early Greeves' would stop, usually thanks to their 197-cc Villiers engines. The noxious Villiers two-strokes were more suited to driving bench saws than powering motorcycles, scramblers or otherwise.

Pundits believed that slag could be turned into diamonds sooner than the 197-cc Villiers could be made into a proper scrambler engine. Such an assessment failed to weigh the talent of Brian Stonebridge, who was yet another brilliant British development engineer. Indeed, Stonebridge emerged as the nearest thing to the mad scientist ever discovered in the British rider-development-engineer clan. He achieved things by himself, on mini-budgets, that would take whole factories years to unlock. At BSA he used discarded parts to build a 250 two-stroke racer, which turned out about two-thirds the horsepower generated by the corresponding project on BSA's experimental stocks. Stonebridge ignored the pointed comments about his underachieving engine. He just went out and rode roughshod over a field of 500's.

During one company bloodletting in 1957, BSA slashed its competition commitments and booted Stonebridge out, whereupon he trotted over to join Bert Greeves. His intention was to put Greeves' scrambling into the major leagues, which meant "developing" something out of nothing with the Villiers engine. The addition

from zero came quickly. Stonebridge was able to get 14 hp out of an enlarged 197-cc Villiers engine, and with it he drummed the 500's in the Allcomers showing. Before he was finished, the basic Villiers engine had become part Greeves with special cylinder heads and altered port shapes. Later, Greeves machines were fitted with big square-finned alloy barrels—hard-chromed by the German Mahle process—and special exhaust plumbing, shorter and fatter forerunners of the long-taper expansion chambers. Greeves even built two engines (197 and 250 Villiers-based units) in two states of tune: one for hard, fast circuits, the other for slower, muddy going.

Stonebridge campaigned in the 1958 and 1959 European Championships, getting close to grabbing the 1959 title before an injury sidelined him. Later that year an automobile accident took his life, a bitter blow that knocked a hole in Greeves' motocross fortunes. But as a memorial to the Stonebridge genius, the Greeves motocrossers raced on, taking Dave Bickers to victories in the 1960 and 1961 European Championship.

If the Stonebridge-developed Greeves' could put away 500-cc motocross machines in Allcomers scrambling in England, then the big 500 scrambler/motocrossers were doomstruck. That lesson was not lost at BSA, where small four-stroke engines did as much as any two-stroke to hurry the demise of the huge four-strokes. With 350-cc, 420-cc, and 441-cc motocrossers derived from BSA's 350 single-cylinder road machine, Jeff Smith laced together a series of wins which gave him the 1964 and 1965 World Championships in motocross. Smith, who championed weight-saving, introduced an economy of effort into motocross action that offset and partly eliminated physical exhaustion. He path-picked the smoothest, often longest, but invariably the fastest, route around any given motocross track. He appeared to be speeding up as the race progressed, but Smith insisted that the other competitors

197

*Eyes focused on the flag,
bodies poised and tense, front
wheels resting against
the start gate—motocrossers
at Daytona 1973 await
the battle, only a half-instant
away. The starter releases
a flood of color, noise,
and close-quartered action.*

were just going slower. The BSA-Smith combination proved what an alliance of light weight, reasonable power, excellent handling, and reliability could mean in motocross terms. That was a message that two-stroke manufacturers could hardly miss. For no matter how light and compact and powerful a small four-stroke could be, a small two-stroke could be more so.

Two-stroke builders hadn't missed the point. In the 500 class, Vlastimili Valek sneaked a Grand Prix second place on a 263-cc Czechoslovakian CZ. The following year, factory CZ's appeared in 360-cc guise, weighing only 232 pounds, but looking heavier. Complete with big-area finning on the light-alloy barrels, the engine allegedly produced 30 gutty horsepower. The CZ actually had less horsepower than the old semiexotic full 500's, but the Czech bike also weighed far less. Nevertheless, in 1964 the horses kept choking up inside the CZ, as the engine contracted the old two-stroke malady of square pistons inside round barrels: seizure. The experiment of 1964 turned to qualified success in 1965, though BSA still won the world title. By 1966, CZ got its sums right, winning the World Championship and retaining it in 1967. Then Husqvarna's 360-cc two-stroke, from a line dating back to 1963, took a two-year lease on the world title. By this time, weekend racers were prepared to pay hefty sums for effective motocross machinery. So in came Maico, the West German firm, followed by Suzuki and Yamaha, the Japanese. The big two-stroke, 360 cc and up, had become the optimum motocross bike—one combining power, light weight, ease of handling, simplicity, and reliability, all in the correct proportions. For old-fashioned four-strokes, it was good-bye. In motocross, Americans never missed the big four-strokes. The bangers had virtually disappeared by the time some ambitious souls transplanted European motocross to the United States.

In the late 1960's, skeptics could rattle off several reasons which might have made motocross in America a chancy thing. The American Motorcycle Association, the most powerful sanctioning body in the United States, dismissed European motocross with a sniff and a shrug. Genuine European motocross lay outside the American mainstream of racing. (In the U.S., the life spans of other European-cultivated motor sports, such as World Championship road racing, had been unmercifully short.) Private funding and independent organization of a motocross tour invited a disaster, since such efforts were usually long on confusion and short on dollars. And promoters couldn't stage one or two races, but had to commit themselves to a series strung out across the United States.

The prophets of doom gagged on their predictions. A privately sponsored tour by a few European riders sparked at the vital center of a motorcycling public. Combustion seemed spontaneous and continuous, taking the form of repeated annual tours, involvement of the American Motorcycle Association in motocross sport, the blossoming of scores of motocross tracks in the United States, the proliferation of learn-to-motocross schools, an AMA Championship motocross series, and finally the creation of an American slot—the United States Motocross Grand Prix—on the international motocross calendar. Many of the old-time motorcyclists, whose forward vision had always been obscured by large rear-view mirrors, were sorely amazed by the rapid development.

The growth of motocross was nothing short of phenomenal. No one could remember anything quite like it. American mainstream racing—flat-track racing—had traditionally leaned on outside events, such as county and state fairs, for a pool of spectators. By no accident was the fabled 50-Mile National on the Springfield Mile held annually during the Illinois State Fair. But so powerful and immediate was the appeal of motocross, it needed no outside help to sustain it. Quite the opposite started to happen. Motocross events were used to pump up attendance at national road-racing events. At Daytona, America's richest, most star-studded international road race, motocross racing brought as many spectators through the gates as the road racing. In three or four short years talk surfaced about "The Other Daytona." At other tracks, motocross races began in 1970 as fillers—to hold the attention of audiences between road races—and ended as equal attractions. Bulldozers and graders assembled some of these tracks with little time and less concern, and motocross riders came to feel that track owners were exploiting them to draw crowds for road racing.

By 1974, when two people talked about "motorcycle racing" in America, motocrossing very likely was the subject. The motocross rage in the U.S. was a logical spin-off of the American off-road explosion. For motorcycle enthusiasts who concentrate their riding off-road and for those who only dabble there, European (and later American) professionals perform feats with which the everyday rider can identify. He can be close enough to see what happens to the motorcycle and its rider. The race is a school. Even if the casual trail rider's conception of the sport is a quantum leap away from the reality of professional motocrossing, the off-road rider shares threads of common experience with the motocross racer, and he can appreciate the professionals' enormous skills. He appreciates how quickly the racer must be going to jump over a mudhole rather than ride through it, what kind of jolting a body takes with a nose-first landing, how fast the rider must react to save a motorcycle that begins a slide to earth, how weary a body feels behind a face drawn and empty with fatigue.

In contrast, the spectator who watches a road-racing or dirt-track event is not only divorced from the action by some distance, he is separated by experience. Many motorcycle enthusiasts ride on hard pavement, but nothing in the course of street riding would permit the everyday rider to sense the time-and-space compression inherent in a 150-mph approach to an 80-mph corner. Motocross doesn't have such wide blank spaces between racer and off-road rider.

The heart and soul of motocross in the United States is amateur competition. Motocross racing is not only something many spectators watch, it is something they also do. Gone are the old English days in which the amateur unbolted the lights and fenders and scurried into battle. Today the amateur racer buys a lightweight competition machine, built as a motocrosser at the factory. The weekend racer has a wide array of production motocross bikes from which to choose, and every year the range broadens. Almost all motocross bikes are constructed on the single-cylinder, two-stroke format. Whether the rider in interested in a 125-cc, 250-cc, 360-cc, or larger engine, the two-stroke singles dominate.

Others may have arrived first at the motocross, but the Japanese, following the market, jumped into the program just as European makers were strapped to keep pace with demand. The amateur side of motocross would probably have hit a ceiling and stopped growing without the entry of Japanese firms, which kept the pipelines to America filled with machines.

Motocross is an affordable kind of racing which does not filter out amateurs. Motocrossers are the least expensive single-purpose racing machines in motorcycling. That fact does not make motocrossing cheap by any means; however a motocross machine is far less of a financial burden than a road racer. And, fortunately for the weekend racer, motocross motorcycles are relatively simple machines. Baffling complexities there may be, but nothing like the number of variables with which the competitor in road races must deal.

Few American amateur racers ride any motocross machine exactly the way it comes out of its shipping crate. No sooner is the new machine on its wheels than the American enthusiast begins replacing pieces, such as forks and suspension units, and fitting lightweight gear such as accessory tanks and seats. This American impulse is automatic, because most riders hope to build into the motorcycle itself small advantages that will give them an edge on the competition. Motorcyclists, as lovers of nuts and bolts, show a natural inclination to tinker, to modify, to experiment—if not always to improve. Every amateur racer, in the back of his mind, hopes for a machine that will buckle the opposition and carry the day, thus saving the beginner the arduous task of learning his track craft. There is almost a secret-weapon type of mentality to this, a fervent hope that the superiority of nuts and bolts will somehow spare the necessity of enduring, of soldiering through, of doing things the hard, unavoidable way.

European amateurs modify far less than their American contemporaries. They run machinery much as it comes from the crates. Rather than tune up the bike, riders work themselves into better physical shape. In part, the European amateur may not be able to find or afford "trick" pieces. Yet there's more to it. Exposed longer to motocross, European amateurs perhaps know that the beginning stages can't be bypassed. Europeans in general have less faith in the secret-weapon hopefulness which buoys American competitors. Whereas Americans see the difference between close victory and defeat as a difference in machinery, European enthusiasts just as easily credit differences in riders.

For amateur sport to flourish, time and distance boundaries, as much as cost, must be convenient. If not, the hobby can take possession of the enthusiast; and he begins to organize his life around it. At that point amateur sport ends, and nonpaid professionalism begins. Amateur motocross holds things in simple balance. Not only are machines straightforward and comparatively inexpensive, but races are near and often—on tracks that sprout up with heartening regularity. Motocross doesn't demand that the weekend racer turn his life upside down to become an active competitor.

Amateur motocross normally pushes older riders toward the rear. The white-collar, over-twenty-five generation likely gravitates to the mid- and lower field, wherein civil servants and lawyers battle dentists and insurance salesmen. Motocross racing is one of the last preserves of ritualized violence, but since it is done with machines rather than guns, the nature of the thing might go unnoticed. American football is violent on a one-to-one human level. Motocross racing, more refined, is one step removed. The object is to pass the next fellow without stuffing him into the turf. And as reward for the stepped-up pace, the rider's own machine hammers him all the more. At least to a certain stage, the faster and better you are, the more you may be in pain. Physical conditioning can harden the rider, minimizing and postponing fatigue. But American amateurs shrink from hard physical training, and that leaves youngsters as the competitors who are naturally in the best condition for motocross.

Make a small mistake and you pay a price in motocross, loss of a place or two. The difference between thirty-second and thirty-third might at first seem insignificant, but not for the weekend racers, whose struggle for thirty-second place leaves them unaware of the first thirty places. Big mistakes extract more than mental anguish. A split-second's loss of concentration can plant a motocrosser face down and spreadeagled in one of those muddy lakes that invariably occupy a large section of any motocross track. Such mud is not necessarily soft, especially when contact occurs with a resounding splat at 25 mph.

Near the front, amateur motocross tends to be under-twenty-five racing. That's not surprising, given the

*Swedes, Germans, British,
Spanish, Italians, Czechs, Austrians,
Canadians, Mexicans, Taiwanese,
and Japanese—all build motocrossers.
It is the most international
side of motorcycling. Those vast
production lines end with
a patch of sunlight, a blur of color,
and a happy brapping sound.*

physical demands. That there are so many adolescents in motocross racing should hardly be startling, either. Americans motorize their offspring at an early age. Minibikes and minicycles hide behind many suburban garage doors. The machines come out in late afternoons and weekends, disappearing into field and wood. Instead of electric trains and Erector sets, affluent youngsters grow up on scaled-down two-wheelers. Long before they reach their majority age for street motoring, small boys have already pressed toward their riding limits in the dirt. Youngsters, fairly durable despite tumbling, don't carry any pervasive sense of the impossible. While experience is a great teacher, inexperience can likewise educate. In any event, eleven-year-old trail-hounds soon enough become fourteen-year-old motocrossers, quick at picking up and imitating fast riders, and unburdened by most of the things a thirty-year-old must unlearn.

Youth and rabid interest can ring up quick results. The amateur ranks produce an entire group of professional motocross stars between the ages of sixteen and twenty. Behind the American crash program stand the Japanese factories which keep the off-road and motocross riding ranks supplied with equipment, and whose bankrolls support an army of young professionals. The Japanese did not create professional motocross racing either in Europe or the United States. They did, however, raise the operating and winning stakes, and with more money came greater opportunities for professionalization of the sport.

The money brought a new degree of internationalization to motocross, too. Professional European riders trip off to the United States to ride in American series, and some Americans go to Europe to try the World Championship series there. Jim Pomeroy, a young American rider for the Spanish Bultaco factory, won the 250-cc round of the Spanish Motocross Grand Prix in 1973. That same year, West German Willi Bauer topped the United States Motocross Grand Prix with a German Maico, Belgian Roger De Coster won the 500-cc World Championship on a Japanese Suzuki, while Hakan Andersson from Sweden captured the 250-cc world title on a Japanese Yamaha. The crisscross of international racing continues season after season.

Motocross has preserved truly amateur racing, kept the fun in motorcycle racing, and provided youthful racers with a consuming interest. That's how motocross began, and despite its trappings of international business, motocross has stayed faithful to its origins. Somehow, as you watch an insurance salesman and a lawyer struggling with mud, ruts, sand, and jumps, putting up with sweat, sore muscles, fatigue, and numbness, while dicing for a prize no less grand than thirty-second place, you know those chaps who organized the first Southern Scott Scramble would have understood and approved.

the mechanics

Racing motorcycles live hard and die easily. Long stretches of inactivity connect to short bursts of terrific abuse. Racing machines spend hours—even days—packed away inside trucks and vans which speed along the American interstate highways. The vast yawning expanses separating major professional races in the United States dictate long grinding hauls. Through the windshield of a transporter, you can see a changing landscape run beyond the green-and-white interstate signs. Sitting in the truck, or driving it, hour after hour, resembles suffering through twenty hours of home movies. In the early morning light the world sneaks out of the cold grayness in three dimensions. A half-hour later color seeps into the windshield movie. By early afternoon a brilliant sun overexposes the screen, then rain-puckered clouds intercept the sun and douse the theater in waving sheets of water. Shortly thereafter the sun burns itself out in the rear-view mirrors and only the headlight beams release the concrete highway and its green signs from the clutches of another night.

No one in motorcycle racing has escaped these long journeys. Now, at the very top of racing's hierarchy, there are factory-sponsored riders who fly to major events, but the headline riders drove miles and miles long before they flew. The foot soldiers on racing's front line—professional mechanics, private riders, volunteer pit crews—take the great concrete way. When all extra time has been poured into the preparation of the machines, the luxury of an overnight stop, indeed the very possibility of a halt, vanishes. Candy bars, sandwiches, cigarettes, coffee, gas stops, drive-in restaurants, driver-switches, catnaps notch the stages of the trip. And the talk: motorcycle racing, food, music, motorcycle racing, traffic, the lack of a really good fifty-cent drive-in hamburger, motorcycle racing, weather, last year's trip over the same route to the same place, the preparation of the machines, motorcycle racing.

Whether done on a road-racing course, a moto-cross track, or some other field of battle, motorcycle racing extends the attractions of motorcycling to their final limits. There is joy in riding well and going quickly, in that conscious and unconscious communication which joins the road, motorcycle, and rider in one streaming dimension. The machine and the path under it come alive to the rider. An electrifying telegraphy occurs between them at the outer limits. But such intense excitement should not be, cannot be, sustained on the public roads or trails. It is the search for that continuing exhilaration in a reasonable setting which brings most riders, at least in the beginning, to the starting lines at organized racing events.

If competition riders represent the logical conclusion of this telegraphic side of motorcycling, then race mechanics may well symbolize the natural end point of the motorcyclist's passion for things mechanical. Motorcycles seduce lovers of nuts and bolts because they give off such a strong machine-quality. And at bottom, racing motorcycles, thanks to their undiluted single-purposefulness, broadcast their machine-quality in clear, ringing tones. So magnetic are these machines that a careful observer might wonder: Who are the real stars of motorcycle racing—the riders or the machines?

"Mechanic" covers a multitude of individuals who fill out coveralls and bear wrenches. At low-level amateur events, fathers and friends are likely to be drafted into service. Fathers may be willing conscripts since they have a vested interest in the preservation of offspring and equipment. Hours of mechanical duties have been offered and accepted in the name of fun and friendship. At a higher level of competition, race preparation becomes more significant, but unless a considerable amount of money is involved, mechanics are still recruited on a non-paying basis. At the highest level of racing—factory-backed efforts—the rules shift. The larger the bankrolls—and the more critical the winning, the more professional the per-

*Opening pages: An explosive
six-second burst of activity surrounds
Yvon du Hamel's road racer in the pits for
fuel during a 1972 AMA event.
Below: Ray Weishaar, Harley-Davidson's
1920 winner of America's Cornfield
Classic in Marion, Indiana, discusses tread
wear. Narrow tires, inflated to
90 psi, were shellacked to wheel rims.*

Left: In 1919, at the Cornfield
Classic, a circus tent did nicely as a
paddock. With proper wrenching,
those frail motorcycles would average
more than 65 mph for 207 miles.
Below: A 1919 pit stop, which took about
75 seconds and included a change
of wheels, allowed a few brief words
between mechanics and riders.

sonnel—riders and mechanics—become.

In the 1970's, a corps of professionalized mechanics emerged in the United States who looked after the equipment used in American Formula 750 road racing. The ruling moguls of motorcycle factories in Japan, England, and the United States believed that racing was an important means of advertising, and from that belief flowed certain consequences. In an effort to win, factories developed special racing machines, fielded teams of professional riders either directly or through American and European distributors, and maintained an infrastructure designed to support the riders and aid race-by-race development of the machines. There was nothing especially new in this system of racing—European factories had underwritten Grand Prix motorcycle racing for decades, and in the 1960's the Japanese arrived in Europe. The Grand Prix motorcycles of the 1960's were staggeringly complex. Only factory personnel had the resources to keep the bikes running.

In America, domestic manufacturers had followed a less direct method of support, filtering rather simple machines through selected tuners and riders. But by the late 1960's, this informal support system for racing began to fall apart. Winning became a matter of company policy at more factories, and this enthusiasm produced more money for racing, new and more sophisticated equipment, and a new group of professional riders and mechan-

For a mechanic on race weekend, hands are never idle. There is always a tire change, or gear switch, or some kind of small adjustment, whether it be done in the garage area or near the starting line. The pressures never are low, for the stakes are high. In America, winning the AMA Number One Plate, and keeping it, is the game.

ics in America. The change came first and most rapidly in road racing—which was only natural. Of all specialized equipment, road-racing motorcycles are the most intricate machines mechanically, and therefore demand the greatest logistical support, including professional race mechanics.

"Mechanic" suggests something far too simple about those who tend the fastest, most powerful road racers in the world. These individuals do more than troubleshoot, spin wrenches, take motorcycles apart and put them back together again. Perhaps "tuner" is a more suitable word, but tuner is another one of those curiously inappropriate words. It suggests someone who can improve upon the performance of a standard model by careful assembly and adjustment. In the past, when standard models were proper gear for racing in the United States, tuning in the traditional sense may have applied. Once upon a time, a good race mechanic could go about his business with a set of prescriptions—a list of do's and don't's for extracting more power from an engine. Yet the great tuners of bygone days did more than meticulously screw all the parts together. The best tuners, the best mechanics, have always surpassed tuning: They create.

Mechanics are literally the power and reliability behind riders. A great rider might be able to overcome a mediocre motorcycle, but there's no way to compensate for a mediocre mechanic who can reduce a brilliant machine to an erratic one and fill any rider with doubts and anxieties. In order to handle a factory-sponsored machine, the man in the pit must have a creative intellect, not just a problem-solving talent, because solving just one specific problem in a particular channel may trigger changes in other channels, a process which fosters cumulative problems. Without a sense for picking his way through a delicate web of strands, a mechanic can summarily ruin one engine after another, and with them his rider's chances.

The road-racing season in the United States runs almost the year around, but the calendar of national events begins in March and ends in October. A period of two to four weeks normally separates major road races in the United States, so off weekends open up to the top-rank professional riders. They may commute to England to ride important short-circuit events there, or chase over to the Continent and race there.

Mechanics travel less than riders. The machines dominate even their "off-time," especially if those machines happen to be factory-backed racers. It's a stop-and-go life. First, the hectic race weekend, followed by a ride of long, grinding hours inside a truck transporter, a dulling haul, particularly on the homeward leg. Near-total collapse follows the arrival at home base. There's much wisdom in hiding out in bed, if for no other reason than ducking the telephone which rings every time some friend or acquaintance might want a blow-by-blow description of the race weekend. If the truck arrival and ensuing collapse have occurred on a Monday evening, a Wednesday morning return to the world usually seems desirable.

Since racing machines lack the talent to disassemble themselves, save in the most catastrophic of circumstances, the first task of the factory mechanic must be the complete dismantling of the engine. Road-racing motorcycle engines have the durability of all-day suckers. Mechanics tailor the engine's reliability for the distance of the event, trading off reliability to gain power. If the trade-off works well, the rider is left with an engine that runs like a jet for the appointed number of miles, although additional mileage may cause the bike to rattle to a stop with an engine full of metal scrap. Should the trade-off come up short on distance, or should something else fail unexpectedly and prematurely inside the engine, the rider takes a long walk back to the pits. Either way, after the weekend, the racing engine goes to pieces in the race shop.

To the factory race mechanic, a broken engine

*There are few simple tasks
in a paddock garage. Fitting a new
windscreen on a 175-mph racer
demands attention, for even the smallest
detail may hold a loose thread
by which victory could be unraveled.
A bike crashes in practice; the
mechanics are left to make repairs and
replacements—quickly, accurately.*

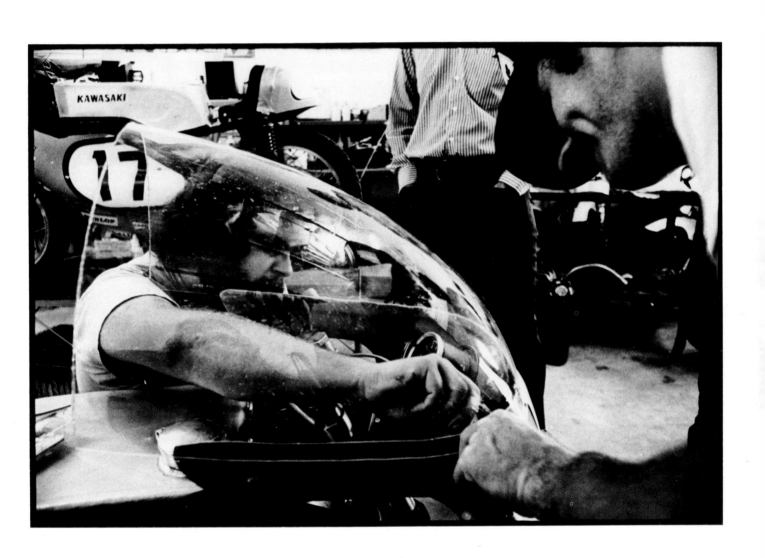

is never as serious as two broken engines, and at times the reserve motorcycle (the stablemate which serves a rider as a back-up machine) may, if the race weekend was especially trying, require a rebuild too. The worst of racing weekends, however, leaves the tuner on a Wednesday morning staring at a crashed and bent motorcycle. Not only does the engine need overhauling, but the entire bike must be rebuilt. The reserve bike might be readied for use, but the first-stringer always incorporates a number of differences in the chassis, and it has all the best components. The race bike reflects every preference, large and small, of the particular rider who uses it. Like Grand Prix cars, the factory-team motorcycles are the same but different, and the pilots' tastes shape those differences.

Whatever Wednesday morning might bring, generally not more than two machines—the race bike and the spare—face the mechanic. Rider and mechanic generally constitute the basic working unit, and ideally the pair should match or complement each other in terms of temperament and personality, since the fortunes and adversities of racing stress any human connection. The rider of a factory racer doesn't necessarily frequent the racing shop where his machine is being assembled during the weeks between the races. Once off the course, the racing machines belong to the mechanic; the rider needn't see his motorcycles until the next test or practice session. And between the last race and the next there stands an awesome amount of work.

Some mechanics have all parts awaiting them on spotlessly clean surfaces, under blinding lights, in an antiseptic room that approximates the clean-room conditions of a space center. But most mechanics don't work that way, at least for long. Parts, tools, and papers encroach upon the workbench space, and eventually the working area comes to resemble a giant amoeba engulfing everything. Then only a sharp, decisive campaign against disorder will restore enough working space in which to proceed with the operation.

The dark hour for a mechanic comes when a racing engine has just been disemboweled; the interior pieces are coated with lubricant and an unpleasant mixture of track oil and dirt covers the external surfaces. Any pistons with holes in the tops, or any folded-over connecting rods heighten the tuner's discomfort. But that dark hour turns its blackest when no parts are on the shelves to substitute for the broken pieces on the work-bench. In theory at least, only private owners and teams regularly experience this cruel moment. Factory-supported efforts are supposed to have parts off the shelves in never-ending streams. Reality does damage to that theory, because there are parts—and then there are parts. Since the works-supported teams experiment first with the latest goods from the factories, and since these highly experimental parts are built in tiny batches someplace an ocean away, those parts bins which serve a factory rider can be bare —not necessarily of all parts, but just the latest ones. That can be critical, because the latest components may hold the winning edge in power, or provide a measure of new reliability which could mean the difference between walking and racing to the finish.

When assembling a racing engine, nothing should escape the mechanic's studied gaze. For example, small cracks can appear in the crankcases. Undetected, the cracking can spread until the engine finally destroys itself with a bang. Every tooth of every transmission gear must be scrutinized. Mechanics try to spot little pits in the mating surfaces, since those pits signal the beginning of the end for the gear. If ignored, the gear tooth may eventually break off—and broken transmission teeth inside a motorcycle traveling at 175 mph can be lethal. With that sobering thought in mind, and a few others like it, the mechanic carefully assembles the gearbox, and, relying on last year's

215

*Above: A factory mechanic
may meet some problems with a kind of
band-aid expediency, such as a fast
track-side welding job. Engine disasters
are clearly beyond recouping.
Right: Motorcycle racers, both the
privateer and factory types,
spend long hours in vans, driving these
transporters and householding in them.*

Opposite: Detailing work continues right up to the starting line. A mechanic scrutinizes every assemblage, wondering where a failure-point might be. Right: The starter holds 3-minute-to-start sign. Scrutiny passes to hope.

notes on the circuit, he arranges the staging between the gears to suit the upcoming racecourse. Every major component—gearbox, engine, suspension units, tires—has to be adjusted and tailored to the requirements of the next racecourse and to the rider's habits, likes and dislikes, riding strengths and weaknesses.

The morning rushes toward noon. Uncrate a new crankshaft. Answer the phone. Talk to a private tuner in need of information. While at the phone, call the team manager and inquire about experimental pistons being jetted in from Japan. True the new crankshaft inside of one hour. Replace all oil seals. Check the transmission shimming. Take another phone call. Install the crankshaft and transmission set into the upper crankcase-half. Make another shifting check. Tap the lower crankcase-half into position. And break for lunch. Ignore the ringing phone on the way out the door. Then wonder if it's an important call. Turn around, start for the phone which immediately stops ringing. Adjourn.

Most mechanics welcome breakaway time from the chore of engine building. Assembling a racing engine is like putting the same jigsaw puzzle together again and again. No matter how tedious the routine becomes, the tuner must be painstakingly—almost surgically—careful. The tedium dare not dull the precise care. Nothing can be put together without close inspection, measurement, computation, and perfect sizing. It is as if all the jigsaw pieces had to be individually filed and honed in order to fit with great precision. That kind of work makes a mechanic a hearty eater and a good cafe conversationalist. At times an hour of irreplaceable time is sold for a self-indulgent reprieve with friends. An hour might be swapped away, but an entire afternoon can't be. The factory mechanic should never allow himself to be worked into a corner by time. Time, or the lack of it, can't be the controlling factor in his preparation of the racing machine. The work at hand should govern the time.

One day can pass into the next week before pistons and cylinders are sized, pistons checked and modified, cylinders and cylinder heads assembled atop the crankcases, compression volumes measured and matched, the engine installed in the frame, the shift mechanism,

*Great mechanical cataclysm
arrives with a shattering finality.
All the parts, so painstakingly
put together, become scrap
metal in a single instant at 9,500 rpm.
Yet there's no time to fret—
only time to build another
engine, believing that
better days indeed lie ahead.*

line, and he is less well equipped to improvise with his own parts than is the full-time factory mechanic who has more experience, better facilities, and greater understanding of what's going on inside the engines.

Among privateer racers, most of what passes for a body of knowledge about a specific racing model is the shared experience of the many who have had an enormous number of things happen to their motorcycles under different circumstances. Much sifting and winnowing of the information must occur before anything can reliably be known. Those who prepare and tune factory-supported motorcycles receive their information in much more systematic ways.

Every privateer comes to believe that the best information collects under the paddock roofs that cover the factory teams. Whether in the paddock or on the telephone, all parties badger the factory mechanic for information. Information descends on a trickle-down basis, but the trickle varies. Factory teams uncover a new bit of knowledge which oozes from the official team to privateers running similar machines. Knowledge which relates to simple reliability travels more quickly than information which pertains to increased engine output. The downward flow travels more freely toward the end of a racing season than at the outset, when all secrets may be sealed airtight. Knowledge about significant power increases tends to trickle at a retarded rate all season long.

Tuners enjoy an abstracted form of racing. They see a race as a battle of concepts and ideas; racing becomes a contest not of men or riders, but of hardware. In gross, unrefined form—close to the viewpoint of the manufacturers—this notion holds that racing is simply a test between major brand names which go to battle with different kinds of equipment; the margin of victory is earned by the superiority of a given piece of racing equipment. This concept of winning is held by many spectators and race followers. However, as understood by mechanics, the hardware theory is far more sophisticated, refined, and subtle. At the very top there are a dozen or so riders capable of winning a major event, so within the limits of human control and the mechanic's hands, racing is the assemblage of all the best combinations for any given course at given times, everything from carburetion to tires to suspension. All variables link together interdependently. An adjustment in one corner may move other adjustments slightly. For the mechanic it is like playing a complex, multidimensional game of tic-tac-toe, or trying to get a long chain of lock tumblers to line up, some of which he can see, and some of which he can't. The pleasure is in finding—sometimes guessing—the combination and then dialing that combination into a machine. In a way, the rider and mechanic work like a safe-cracking team. The mechanic tries to figure out the final combination, but the rider possesses the knob-turning talent and skill.

For the mechanic, racing is an ongoing experiment with equipment, with each attempt marked by success or failure. For him, the race hasn't quite the absolute finality it has for the rider. No matter how intimately connected with the racing effort, the mechanic remains in a realm intellectually—if not emotionally—distant from the actual physical race. It yields more information, more material, more possibilities for future combinations. Riders race each event to completion; mechanics talk it to an end. The last race never ends until the vans bounce through the paddock gates for the next event.

On race weekend, most factory mechanics are in an alert and stimulated state, thanks to adrenalin and coffee. Working in the pits, they try to get basic carburetion and gearing adjustments done before the professional riders show up to take the motorcycles out in early-morning practice sessions. It pleases professional riders to see the factory machines complete and ready to go for practice sessions. Even when there's plenty of time for the mechanic to finish the job, riders get a bit edgy just standing around and seeing the time that the work takes. Mechanics must be trackside psychologists, somehow conveying the impression that the only life the machine lives is the one on the track, under the rider. That other part of the machine's existence—in the paddock garage or the racing shop at home base—is something the rider can do without. He doesn't want to know how much trouble the motorcycle gave going together, and he's not interested in a rundown on the snags of rebuilding. The rider's mind points toward the race, and no room exists for much of anything else. The rider's success depends upon the machine's perfect health and operation, and seeing the device under prolonged treatment in the paddock—or hearing about it—only raises doubts in his mind.

All information must be recorded. There may be so many changes that nothing can be trusted to memory: carburetion settings, ignition timing, compression ratio, tire compounds and pressures, gearing, and more. The factory mechanic must know where he started. Otherwise he could wander around in tuning circles. Since factory bikes are updated race-to-race with the latest engine pieces, the machines require abundant information gathering. And that material only can be determined experimentally in practice sessions.

When his motorcycle is out in a practice session, the mechanic can't withdraw to some quiet corner. His eyes and ears seek out his machine. From the pits he can hear the heaviness in the exhaust note of an over-jetted machine, or pick up a sparkplug misfire easily. If everything sounds perfect, there are still lap times to track and record. When the practice session closes and the rider returns with the machine, the mechanic has to know tachometer readings at given places on the circuit, the quality of midrange acceleration, the behavior of the bike over bumps in fast, sweeping bends, and dozens of other bits of information. Between professional rider and mechanic, there's an economy of words before and after practice sessions. The information from the morning practice session allows the combination to be further refined. The mechanic works quickly to reset the machine with the greatest possible precision. The late-afternoon practice session gives an opportunity to check the revised settings. Another seven or eight laps. Another conference. A determination of the final settings for tomorrow's race. The mechanic compiles his last preparation list, first in his head, then on paper.

After the late afternoon session, the factory riders leave the paddock area. Mechanics take a rain check on an early dinner, for the factory machines must be torn down, checked and reassembled. Heads, cylinders, and pistons come off. The parts are studied for colors and marks which indicate spot-on running or signal potential trouble. Check, and check, and check. Item by item, the list shortens. It's back to fighting off tedium, back to honing and polishing jigsaw pieces, with no thought of taking a break. Final engine assembly ties off a day already going to darkness.

As daylight fails, the mechanic's world shrinks. First the whole track area drops away, leaving the lighted garage and finally just the driver's seat of the truck, the glow of the instruments, and the patch of the road ahead that leads back to the motel. For two weeks the mechanic's energies have channeled and narrowed toward the starting grid. At the starting line, the machine belongs to the rider. The mechanic's days of building and hours of adjustment have passed.

After a late dinner in his room, the factory mechanic can have a shower, make a phone call or two, and then wind tomorrow into the alarm clock and try to make up for lost sleep.

12.

essay on a champion

Halcyon days returned to motorcycling with the opening of the 1970's. Not since the days preceding World War I had motorcycling been so alive, so prosperous, and so international. The American scene burgeoned in the 1960's. European motorcycling resurged in the 1970's. From Japanese factories, machines poured out to the Orient, Europe, and the Americas.

The motorcycle world that bought together, raced together. The United States no longer hung isolated with a particular set of competition rules that ignored motorcycle racing abroad. And "international" racing no longer meant British and Europeans racing against one another. The Yanks had arrived, and so had the Japanese. Motorcycle racing wasn't evenly homogenized throughout the world; national differences remained. Yet most American enthusiasts would instantly recognize stars like Roger De Coster and Joel Robert and Giacomo Agostini, while European observers knew such names as Jim Pomeroy and Calvin Rayborn and Hideo Kanaya.

Consider Kel Carruthers. In his native Australia, a teen-aged Kel built his own road-racing special. Later, in his twenties, he left for the European Grand Prix circuits as the most successful rider in Australia. In Europe, he won the 250 World Championship on an Italian Benelli and defended his crown the next year on a Japanese Yamaha. Then Carruthers transferred his business to the United States where his road-racing success was instantaneous, demonstrating that at the very top, racers were racers the world around.

Kel Carruthers would disappoint those who might hold a stereotyped view of the motorcycle racer. In a world grown remote from immediate physical dangers, some armchair philosophers might assume that high-risk activities automatically become the pursuits of fools and idiots, and that professional racing is fit work for senseless knaves who are all muscle and reflexes, and who

scramble monosyllabic words. What a shock to this conception is Kel Carruthers, an articulate businessman. If motorcycling became serious business in the 1960's, so did racing, and Carruthers grew with the sport.

French's Forest Trial, 1950, Northern Districts' Motorcycle Association, Australia: Sandwiched in the report of the *Free Motorcycle Weekly* was an item. "Mention must be made of the riding of 12-year-old Kelvin Carruthers, son of Jack Carruthers, who rode his Royal Enfield through all sections with the loss of 48 points. The Champion of the Future?" Jack Carruthers was a motorcycle dealer in Sydney, Australia, and when Kel was twelve, Jack bought his son a little 125-cc, three-speed, hand-shift Royal Enfield. Legally, Kel was much too young to ride his machine on the street and he couldn't go dashing off into the Australian wilds without using the public roads. He suffered the common dilemma of all young motorcyclists —enthusiasm and equipment, but no place to ride. The solution developed shortly enough. Kel went along to motorcycle events with his father, and he adapted quickly and easily to riding his new motorbike in competition.

Kel continued to compete on motorcycles, perhaps out of that natural inertia that keeps individuals doing what they have discovered they do well. One falls into soccer playing naturally, and motorcycle competition as a sport isn't much different. Inclinations and preferences for motor racing pointed Carruthers off in a slightly different direction from his classmates. His early exposure to motorcycle racing consumed a great deal of time. While other twelve- and thirteen-year-olds were out cricketing, Kel was engine-tinkering or off to a race meet.

Kel worked in his father's motorcycle business and at fifteen he joined the business full-time. Australians believe that individuals should get on with the task of making a living early in life, an attitude that works nicely in a country with immense underdeveloped resources, vast

Opening pages: The starting grid at Road Atlanta, 1973. A relaxed body and quizzical face suggest a man beginning to focus his entire concentration on the upcoming road race. Below: A burst of yellow and black identifies Kel Carruthers and his Yamaha, at one and at speed.

space, and relatively few people. The Australian school system encourages young men to finish school at fifteen and begin a useful trade education. And so Kel found himself in the motorcycle trade; it was a logical place for him to be. Racing? He raced for fun, for there was nothing else but fun in local motorcycle racing.

Much of Australian motorcycle racing took place on twisting dirt courses about a mile in length. There were a few good paved circuits, such as Bathurst, which had been constructed in 1937, but most macadam circuits were built later. When young Carruthers began racing, organizers simply laid out hard-surfaced courses on abandoned or unused air fields. Most Australian riders raced on dirt and paved road courses. Although speedway, motocross, observed trials, and grass-track racing all made up part of the Australian racing scene, any serious young racer learned to handle himself on the twisting courses, both paved and unsurfaced.

Sometimes a young racer could have problems just getting on a track. Kel made his open competition debut when he was fifteen years old. "Open" meant that an event was open to riders outside the sponsoring club's membership. Young Carruthers drew attention, not only because he rode his BSA Bantam quite well in his home-club events, but also because his open competition license stirred a controversy. The Auto-Cycle Union in Australia required that its open license applicants be licensed street motorcyclists, and this requirement foiled Kel, who was too young for a regular driving license. It mattered little that he was already a veteran competitor and quite able to deal with older, more experienced racing motorcyclists. Rules were rules.

But motorcyclists have always been an enterprising lot. After all, British scrambling began in a squabble over ACU rules. Father Jack and son Kel figured their way around the licensing problem. With help from the

Australian army, the Carruthers team secured a special road-test license for young Kel, since the Carruthers concern serviced the army's Harley-Davidsons.

Kel won his competition license. His performance on the racetrack seemed to justify the license maneuvering. During his first year of open competition, Kel notched eleven wins, one fourth, one sixth, and one dnf (did-not-finish). His new license—and his 125-cc Bantam, 350 BSA, and 500-cc Ariel—had served him well.

In his sixteenth summer, Kel ran a BSA 350 single, which was a pure Carruthers special, developed out of his rigid-framed BSA dirt bike. He practically invented the machine, which had an iron BSA engine, Royal Enfield frame, and Norton gearbox.

Building a race machine in Australia in the early to mid-1950's was not an operation which could be farmed out to an army of specialists. One couldn't trundle off to the local machine shop with cylinder head in hand and have the ports carved out to known racing specifications. The engine builder consulted his own thin library of speed-tuning manuals, decided what or whom to believe, and proceeded to whittle away in his own workshop. Nor, generally, could the builder thumb through a vast catalogue of racing parts and order up a racing camshaft. If you wanted a special camshaft, then you cleared a set of hurdles: You researched cam design, pored over perplexing alternatives, actually found a way to grind a camshaft —and then you did it. The process wasn't easy, but then the builder learned more about racing camshafts than a series of parts-order numbers. High-compression racing pistons might be bought off accessory shelves, but they were not exactly ready for installation. The tuner selected rough castings without ring grooves or rings, and worked forward from there. Jack and Kel Carruthers spent hours and hours turning out special pieces for the BSA in their small machine shop.

If one reads history backward, one might conclude that Kel Carruthers wasted a good deal of racing time in the late 1950's. When he was ready for a genuine production racer, Kel was still fiddling with his Bantam and the 350 BSA creation. Had he spent all his time between the ages of eighteen and twenty-one developing his racing talent, Carruthers might have speeded his career. But hindsight skews the past. In reality, by his twentieth birthday Kel Carruthers had yet to decide to be a professional motorcycle racer.

He took a wife in the summer of 1957, and he and Jan, like many other young Australians, immediately looked forward to raising a family. From 1954 to 1960, Kel was a reasonably successful racer who ran for the sport of it. He managed to do only about ten races a season, most of which were in New South Wales and fairly close to home. Racing was never a do-or-die proposition for Carruthers, who was young and energetic fellow building a secure future based on business and family.

1961 was a pivotal year in Carruthers' racing career. When Honda began its assault on Grand Prix racing, the Japanese concern created new opportunities for many racers, including Kel Carruthers. Honda built six 250-cc, four-cylinder racing machines for the sales department to use for promotional purposes, a move which dovetailed with their major thrust in European road racing. The promotional bikes were show replicas of the works racers, with chrome exhaust pipes and carefully applied paint. Honda sent one of the show replicas to the Australian Honda importer, Bennett and Wood. The factory also sent a spare engine and a few extra parts, and Japan asked the Australians to find a competent rider for the machine. Bennett and Wood found Carruthers.

The Honda was the best piece of racing equipment on the continent, but the machine was not as good as one might imagine. True, the four-cylinder engine developed 42 hp, a shattering number for a 250 at the time, and the power ran to the rear wheel through a six-speed gearbox, certainly a generous number for 1961. There the good news ended. The bike had an extraordinarily short wheelbase, and the frame flexed in every conceivable direction, allowing the bike to gallop and lurch through corners. Although Kel modified the frame, his work only eased the intensity of the cornering antics. Despite its unruly nature, the basic superiority of the machine and the Carruthers talent devastated both the 250-cc and 350-cc classes.

Very swiftly in 1961 Carruthers became professionalized. He could no longer race at his own leisure. Honda wanted the four-cylinder machine raced outside Carruthers' own locale, so the years of ten-races-per-season belonged to the past. To fill out his expanded racing schedule, Carruthers campaigned a CR-93 Honda production racer in the 125-cc class, and in the 500-cc division he used a Manx Norton. Success created a snowball effect: The more he raced, the better he became, the more he won, the stronger the encouragement, the greater his commitment to racing. Kel ended the five-year period from 1961 to 1965 as Australia's number-one rider. He chalked up 115 wins, 27 seconds, 7 thirds, and 4 fourths in 161 starts. After the Bathurst races in May, 1965, *Wheels* concluded that "Kel Carruthers was so far out in front that they almost reopened the road before the rest of the field turned up."

A racer can drift toward a decision or rush up on it. But the time arrives when a racer can no longer be carried forward by the natural current of events. By 1963, Kel Carruthers had reached a portage point. He had won everything worth winning in Australia; he could only begin to turn in circles—a perfectly pleasant maneuver if he wanted to end his career in Australia. To grow in the racing business, he had to pick up his entire life, move halfway around the world, and take a calculated gamble

Top: Kel, left, and (clockwise) Ralph Bryans, Phil Read, Mike Hailwood, and Bill Ivy chat at Sachsenring in 1967. Center: As Jan trims away on Paul, Kel assembles a 350-cc Aermacchi special at Cesenatico, Italy, in 1968. Bottom: At Alicante, Spain, Read leads Kel through streets lined with bags and bales.

on succeeding in the European Grand Prix theater. He couldn't drift into the European scene; unlike the four-cylinder Honda, Europe was not going to come to him.

He wanted to go to Europe as early as 1963, but Jack Carruthers cautioned that Kel's real future might well belong in Australia. Kel was in his mid-twenties. He had a wife and two small children, Sharon and Paul. The family motorcycle business was on the threshold of renewed expansion. All good reasons for staying, but Kel made his decision: professional racing—in Europe.

When the Carruthers' decided to go, they were well prepared. Kel had accumulated enough money to go racing first class with the best equipment available to a privateer. He and Jan could not dash off to Europe on a one-year foray. No one became a first-year sensation, so any hope for professional success rode on at least a two-year program. Once Kel decided to try Europe, Jack supported him completely. Father and son began putting a set of three bikes into as-new condition and shipped them off to England. Kel leased his house; Jack, who went to Europe in 1966, found a friend to live in his.

Arriving in England two months before the racing season began in 1966, Carruthers endured a period of frustration. He had been the champion in Australia, but that didn't count in Europe. He was just another hopeful from faraway trying to break into professional racing. The commitment to Europe was enormous, and so were Carruthers' headaches.

First seasons in Europe make the new racer a victim of an information explosion. Carruthers had to learn the best routes to the racecourses, where to buy parts at the best prices, and the intricacies of red-tape tangles at European customs houses. He spent two days on the Spanish border because the *carnets* he had been using everywhere else were not good there. Had he asked someone about that peculiarity, most likely he would have

gotten a direct answer. But he didn't know that he should ask about *carnets* and the Spanish border.

Most of all Carruthers had to adapt to—and master—Europe's fast, long, natural circuits, which were unlike anything he had ridden before. At Francorchamps there's a fast, wide-radius turn at the bottom of a flat-out downhill section. Experienced riders take the corner tucked in behind the fairing, without slowing down. During Kel's first practice session, he would come down the hill at 145 mph or so on his 500 Manx Norton, sit up, click back a gear, and watch everyone go by him. By race time, he could hurtle through the corner in top gear, hugging the bike, but he would still pop his head up for a quick look. The following season, while dicing in the race with John Cooper and Peter Williams, the threesome would sweep around the corner abreast, chins on the tank, wishing the bikes would go faster.

Natural circuits spell natural dangers: trees, stone walls, light posts, gates, hedgerows, curbstones, manhole covers—just for openers. The omnipresent fixtures brook no fools. The professional rider races inside a trough; the road forms the floor, the scenery the lethal sides. Make a mistake, brush the countryside blurred on the side of the trough, and you pay dearly.

European Grand Prix riders, compared to short-circuit racers in England or America, take few falls. The continental racer can't physically afford costly errors. He races with a calculated conservatism. He won't go chattering into a hairpin, because the time he might gain charging the hairpin is insignificant compared to taking a 120-mph bend perfectly. Carruthers always reckoned it was better to go just as fast as he could without falling off instead of going fast enough to win the race. Eventually, going fast enough to win was the same speed as going fast without falling.

His shrewdness served him well in the start-

233

money game. Organizers of Grand Prix races pay the racers to show up and start in races. The actual amount is subject to offer and negotiation. A racer has to determine how much he's worth to himself, and then figure how much he might be worth to a given race organizer. If an aspiring but unknown racer asks too much, the organizer might cheerfully bump him from the program rather than quarrel. If the racer asks too little, he has cheated himself and made it more difficult to get his true value later. High or low, negotiations can be on-going: offer, counteroffer, haggle, and niggle.

For Carruthers the start-money game was serious down to the last Swiss franc. Kel had traveled thousands of miles to race, invested a great deal of seed money in the venture, and had no desire to stage a going-out-of-business sale in Europe. Kel knew that half the privateers racing in Europe would fail because they lacked the riding, business, or organizational talent to succeed. For a large number of privateers, racing in Europe was something of a holiday, so they came racing on the cheap and had a good time. But one couldn't learn the ins-and-outs of Grand Prix racing by running crippled bikes, nursing along old transporters, or sleeping in ditches.

Kel Carruthers' first season in Europe—1966—was the absolute bottom of his career. The poor results and the unsettling dislocations of life would have been worse without a family to sustain him. They gave him the kind of support not found outside close families. Jan helped enormously. She was Kel's business and pit manager; all correspondence with organizers started and ended at her desk. During the races she took care of three stop watches, gave Kel signals, and decided what information he should have and when he should get it. And on top of it all, she ran the traveling household.

The European racing season opens in April and runs to September. There are early warm-up races in Italy, then a full schedule of Grand Prix events counting for the world titles; important national events, such as the post-TT races, ensue, and—after the Grand Prix season closes—come big-money finales such as the Race of the Year. Professional racers are like field hands; they follow the harvest and lead a mobile wayfaring life. This traveling troupe of racers and their support crews live and work in Europe under the label of the Continental Circus. The name probably comes from the early days of racing when the riders stayed in tents at the circuits, but today's train of vans and caravans on the European roads provides reinforcement for the circus image.

The paddocks become home to the racers when they're not actually going down the road. They leave one circuit and drive directly to the next to set up their equipment for the coming event. One drives straightaway into the paddock, parks his caravan, unloads the machinery, sets up housekeeping, and begins work on the bikes. There's always time to visit with racing friends whose caravans are stationed nearby. Wives and girl friends pile into automobiles and drive off to the local markets to stock up on food and drink. There's a cup of tea at every hour on the hour in someone's trailer, and usually there's a free hand to help if you're stuck on an equipment problem.

When someone in the caravan tribe is killed or seriously injured, everyone shares the grief with those closest to the fallen rider. But there's no time for prolonged mourning. If disaster occurs at Imatra in Finland, one can be driving to Brno in Czechoslovakia two days afterward. A relentless schedule and changing landscapes fill the time and blunt the pain. The circus just travels on, though an unhappy event is never quite left behind.

Good times, bad times, frustration, joy, disappointment, luck, and things much less—Carruthers weathered it all through the 1967 and 1968 seasons. To succeed, to excel, to be noticed—these were the hopes. To get a

236

telegram from a manufacturer who would summon the racer to Italy or Japan or elsewhere for contract talks and testing: That was the privateer's dream. The freshman class of the Continental Circus 1966 contained many members; some had no talent, others lacked organization, many became discouraged, still others ran out of money, maybe a few just changed their minds. Some left the Circus willingly, others unwillingly, a few terminally. Kel Carruthers was the most successful member of the class.

For the Australian, 1969 was a very good year. And an unusual one, too, because Kel rode for two Italian factories at the same time. He raced the first three rounds of the Grand Prix season, the Spanish, French, and West German classics, for Aermacchi in 125-cc, 350-cc, and 500-cc classes. Then—at the Isle of Man—Benelli, with its ranks cut by injuries, recruited Kel Carruthers and Phil Read to race the four-cylinder, four-stroke, 250-cc Benellis. According to team orders, Phil Read was to win if possible; Carruthers was to back him up. But Read and his machine lagged in the race. Despite almost zero practice, Carruthers jetted with his Benelli and won going away.

Victory on the island was one high point for Carruthers and the pale-green Benelli four; others would follow as he stayed on the team. Meanwhile, Kel continued to ride Aermacchis in the other classes, until it looked as if he might win the 250 World Championship. He asked Aermacchi to be excused from riding their bikes so that he could concentrate on the 250 world title. Aermacchi agreed, and Carruthers continued his pursuit, though he still had to ride number-two behind Renzo Pasolini, Benelli's leader. While Carruthers had to defer to Pasolini, the competition was incredibly fierce: Santiago Herrero, a brave and forceful Spanish rider on a single-cylinder, two-stroke Spanish OSSA; the brilliant Swedish newcomer, Kent Andersson, aboard a Yamaha two-stroke twin; Renzo Pasolini, Benelli's number one; and Kel Car-

ruthers, hired by Benelli to backstop Pasolini. The Italian, as team leader, drew the best bikes until a late-season injury sidelined him. Then Benelli pinned all their hopes of a World Championship on Carruthers.

The title rested on the last championship race, the Yugoslavian Grand Prix. Andersson, Herrero, and Carruthers met on the tight Opatija circuit, situated on the Adriatic sea front and the cliffs rising behind it.

Corners down on the sea front would tolerate few mistakes; the left-hander after the start line offered a rock face on the outside and concrete balustrades on the inside. Straw bales, thinly distributed, could no more than soften any crushing blow. The course possessed two near-dead-stop corners—hardly the kind of circuit to match the high-speed preferences of Carruthers or the strengths of the Benelli racer. In 1969, it was tough just getting any sort of grip on the road. The course had been resurfaced and relined only days before the race, and the new paving was slippery, and became even more so when it rained on race days. Racing lines were so slick that one miscue could throw away the World Championship.

Carruthers and Herrero were leading together on the high mountainside of the six-kilometer course when the Spaniard lost his bike—for an instant it seemed that the crashing OSSA might take out Carruthers as well. It didn't. Carruthers recovered, and returned to concentrating on going quickly under miserable conditions. Then the Australian found Kent Andersson's Yamaha tailing the Benelli, almost locked to the Italian bike. Carruthers was under the greatest pressure he had ever known. Andersson pressed him. Carruthers made the supreme effort of his career—rain, slides, wetness, discomfort, concern, concrete posts, solid-rock cliff faces, with Carruthers passing, watching, concentrating, stacking time fractions together, piecing a foot here with another there. In time and distance Carruthers put a margin of victory together. He finished

the race—drained, exhausted, hollow—as the new 250 World Champion.

Carruthers stopped off in the New World early in 1970 in order to buy a set of Yamaha motorcycles for the next Grand Prix season in Europe. He decided to have a peek at American racing, so before winging back to Europe he raced at Daytona. Riding under the Don Vesco banner, Carruthers handily won the 250-cc event. In the 200-mile race, he pushed his 350 Yamaha into contention; then it broke. And so back to Europe Carruthers went, a bit richer for his Florida experience, but still committed to the European racing scene.

The Australian became a privateer again. The Benelli factory deserted the 250-cc class, because an FIM rule change outlawed four-cylinder machines in the 250-cc ranks. In the 350-cc category, Carruthers began the season on an old-model 350-cc Benelli four; strikes and delays prevented the completion of a new and competitive Benelli four. Finally, the Carruthers/Benelli combine broke up, and Kel campaigned his own 350 Yamaha twin. But the 250 class—in which he was defending World Champion—held the most disappointment. Carruthers and his 250 Yamaha led four of the first seven Grand Prix events until the late

stages, and then, in each case, the contact-breakers in the ignition broke. He couldn't buy the electronic systems which factory riders Rod Gould and Kent Andersson used. After all, the Yamaha factory certainly wasn't interested in providing a privateer with the hardware with which to defeat the factory runners. Carruthers succeeded in having an electronic ignition system developed for his twin-cylinder machines, but by then the laws of probability were weighted against him. Rod Gould became the new 250 World Champion.

That bittersweet season of 1970 (runner up in the 250 and 350 World Championships) raised thoughts of retirement in Kel's mind. The gypsy lifestyle with its constant travel was a delightful experiment for the first years, but Kel and Jan Carruthers were becoming weary of the continental grind. Their children were growing up, and raising youngsters on the run didn't agree with Australian sensibilities. The Carruthers' had no real base in Europe, so leaving would be easy.

The racing business might be transplanted. Why not drop by the United States for a season before returning to Australia? America was on the way home. There were fewer than a dozen major road races in the

Pages 238-239: Carruthers leads Gary Fisher at Road Atlanta in 1973. Compared to European circuits, American courses offer wide, safe borders. Left: The Georgia course suits Carruthers' taste more than any other American track. Below: Intense heat makes life inside racing leathers uncomfortable indeed.

United States; the American scheduling would allow a permanent home, if only for a year. And there was money in American racing. It was a good place to set up business.

Their American experiment brought the Carruthers' to the mecca of American motor culture, Southern California. Kel worked out an arrangement with the Don Vesco racing organization and Yamaha International, the American importers of Yamaha motorcycles. Kel developed, tuned, and raced Yamahas under the Vesco standard in the United States.

The American stopover worked. Carruthers was always the man to beat in the 250 races. The American racing rules compelled the 350 Yamahas to run against the 750-cc giants, though the mismatch wasn't as great as the disparity in displacement might suggest. The Road Atlanta race weekend in 1971 made the point. Carruthers scored a double, taking his 250 to the winner's circle after the lightweight race, and returning somewhat later with his Yamaha 350 which captured the big bike race.

Road Atlanta comes as close to a European road circuit as any racing course in the United States. It's a fast, open course. The pavement whips over and around hills, moving left and swerving right in a dazzling set of combinations. The course demands that a rider slice his way around with great precision. Losing concentration muffs not just one corner, but loses time through a series. The course does not yield to hard-charging frontal assaults; it rewards unfailing finesse.

American racing brought Carruthers up against fresh, brash, young riders who rode over their heads and beyond their experience, hoping that they could learn to cope before their next get-off. To experienced eyes, these young racers looked like accidents racing down the road, jockeying for a crash site. The nature of professional road racing in America, Carruthers discovered, encouraged young riders to search for shortcuts to winning speed.

In the first place, results interest Americans far more than progress; no one pays notice to "comers" in American racing—only to winners. In contrast, the European interest extends downfield beyond current winners; with so much to learn about so many continental courses, the sheer volume of necessary knowledge tends to slow beginners until they learn the circuits. Second, with no start money in America, finishing results determine payments, and the better placed a rider is, the more handsomely he is rewarded. In Europe, such a system would starve out most of the Continental Circus. Third, American racing, compared to the Europe form, is short-exposure racing. With few national road races, a young American racer has very few opportunities to be noticed, and he makes the most of these brief exposures. Finally, American courses permit crashes without grim penalties. American racecourses are hardly wonderful places to ditch equipment, but wide dirt shoulders make better landing areas than stone walls.

Carruthers didn't care much for American road courses outside Road Atlanta, and he liked even less young American riders wobbling through corners on all sides of him. It disturbed him to peel off into a relatively slow corner and then discover some youngster diving deeper into the corner, out of shape with the bike and fouling Kel's line, which followed the classic European pattern (in slower but out faster). The technique of entering corners in order to maximize exit speeds didn't always interest young American riders who had little reverence for classic lines. Carruthers could find Americans trying to go fast on any one of several lines through corners. With thick traffic in corners, a fast rider had to deal with traffic jams constantly and effectively—a fact that cost Carruthers at least one major win in 1971. Still, risk was part of Carruthers' business, and in America he earned the reputation of the fox—wily, shrewd, and quick.

The Australian businessman expanded his operations in America in 1972. Joining directly with Yamaha International, Carruthers oversaw their road-racing effort in the United States. He became both playmaker and coach. As Yamaha's stake in professional racing in America grew, Carruthers' talents for management, racing organization, and trackside development began to overshadow his abilities as a rider. By 1973 the Carruthers paddock regime was something of a cross between America and Europe. Kel was paddock manager, chief mechanic, and engineer. He knew more about the racing equipment and its application than anyone else, and he made all important trackside decisions.

He didn't pass out edicts in the fashion of European teams, because ironclad riding instructions—from anyone—ran counter to American racing and its prize-money system. With team riders, Carruthers' talent and professionalism became his bond: The riders received the best possible equipment and his best advice.

Mechanical work on the racing machines followed strict channels. In order to eliminate interteam rivalry, the normal working unit—one rider with one mechanic—had no place inside the Carruthers garage. Carruthers organized everything on a production-line system. After each race, the mechanics worked as an operating team, treating each machine as a machine, not as the racing arm of some individual rider.

In the Yamaha garage, this system worked because, when necessary, communication between rider and mechanic could be filtered through Carruthers, who from first hand experience knew what phenomenon the rider described and what modifications or adjustments might correct that behavior. The diagnosis might require readjusting the machine, or slightly modifying the racer's style of riding, or both. Nothing about race day could be academic for Carruthers; he had done it all.

Retirement. It is a dread word in the vocabulary of most racers. The exit can leave an individual stripped of his profession and self-identity, vacant and at drift. Not Carruthers. He never faced a blank retirement. With his future tied to management and development, the danger factor in racing increased. It was a simple, logical business decision. Carruthers raced less and less during the 1973 season thanks to his team responsibilities. On the track, his concentration divided between his own performance and that of the team. Steadily, team concerns stole time away. There were fewer practice laps and racing miles. Racing less, and concentrating on racing less, Carruthers' skill might lose its final hone; the edge might not cut so deftly. That potential dullness increased the risk-taking on the racecourse. So the businessman cut his risks and ended his globe-trotting racing career.

The exploits of Kel Carruthers could only have happened in the new age of motorcycling. Traditionally, it has been an insular sport; Carruthers is an internationalist. Never, since the first generation of Cannonball Baker and his brethren, has motorcycling been so interconnected worldwide. In its past the sport has produced reckless heroes, who would toss the hindermost to the devil. Yet the sport has had its cool-headed thinkers, and Carruthers is one who has banked on his wits to take him farther than courage alone can do. In twenty years of racing, he suffered his most serious injury as a sixteen-year-old, and that was a broken wrist.

In the larger sense, Carruthers' international business owes much to the resurgence of motorcycling. That wave carried him out from Australia to Europe, and from Europe to the United States. As motorcycling prospered, Carruthers grew from amateur to professional racer, and from racer to manager. His career has been an affirmation of a vital, burgeoning sport. Good as the old days in motorcycling were, these days are far better.

Photographs in this section by Jaydie Putterman

Picture Credits

248

Index